Graphic
Design
Manual

6.95

Miller - 5/11/77.

# GRAPHIC DESIGN MANUAL

## Principles and Practice

Armin Hofmann

**VNR** VAN NOSTRAND REINHOLD COMPANY
NEW YORK CINCINNATI TORONTO LONDON MELBOURNE

Van Nostrand Reinhold Company Regional Offices:
New York Cincinnati Chicago Millbrae Dallas

Van Nostrand Reinhold Company International Offices:
London Toronto Melbourne

ISBN 0-442-23469-4

**Layout:**
Armin Hofmann, Basle
English version:
D. Q. Stephenson, Basle
All the illustrations contained in this book
are reproductions of studies executed
in the Graphic Course (Fachklasse) of
the AGS, Basle
Photographs:
Max Mathys and Rolf Schröter, Zurich
Esther and Paul Merkle, Basle
Photoklasse AGS, Basle
Hans Isenschmid, Basle
Engravings:
Cliché-Anstalt Schwitter AG,
Zurich

Published by Van Nostrand Reinhold Company
450 West 33rd Street, New York, N.Y. 10001

16 15 14 13 12 11 10 9 8

# Contents

7 Preface, George Nelson
9 Introduction, Armin Hofmann
13 The dot, text
21 The dot, illustrations
15 The line, text
75 The line, illustrations
17 Confrontation, text
31 Confrontation, illustrations
19 Letters and signs, text
45 Letters and signs, illustrations

Despite all our efforts to simplify things – efforts constantly expanding in order to keep abreast of steadily increasing complexity – nothing is very simple any more. Even in the arts, traditionally dedicated to the world of the spirit and the sensibilities, the figure of the artist is hard to see with anything of the old clarity. Like his still-incompatible sibling, the scientist, he has fissioned, so to speak, under the pressures of expanding technology, commercial competition, and the bewildering demands of a fast-changing existence.

The artist, whatever his now specialized label, suffers like the rest of us from the shocks which accompany life in a period of massive transformations. Change is always hard to take, but the scale and speed of transition today frequently become unbearable. It is not easy to find meaning in a world whose outlines – and core – daily become less familiar.

In the new world, a fresh landscape and a different climate are coming into existence. Technology has become the central fact of life. It is making hollow nonsense of assertedly conflicting ideologies, and there is no area of daily life left (and soon there will be no spot on the planet) where its influence is not the controlling one. Under this massive assault, nature – including the human variety – recedes into the background, and the individual is invited to convert himself into a docile component in a system. He is also asked – at the point of a gun, so to speak – to accept the idea that knowledge has become too complex to be embraced, even in the most general way, by any single person. He is told that what he is working on is not an entity but a fragment, and that the final product or outcome is really none of his business. Finally, he is constantly warned by the Cassandras of automation that his present insignificant activities may well be rendered superfluous by the next step forward in technique.

To find human content in this new landscape and climate is the problem which confronts all of us, and the answers are not there to be picked up in the street, as the painters have made very clear in the few years since World War II. This small, special group, more highly sensitized than most to shifts in the human environment, has reacted with unbelievable swiftness and violence, running through a series of styles, "periods" or experiments, for which there is no parallel in the history of art.

It would be easy to evoke, nostalgically and probably inaccurately, images of a simpler time, when the young apprentice went into the studio of the master, learned to grind pigments, to paint backgrounds, to delineate figures in the manner of his teacher, and eventually to deal with the accepted subject matter of his time, such as the classical legends. It would be tempting also to contrast this idealized situation with the one presented by this book, which says in effect, "there is no acceptable subject matter in art". In fact, there is no longer agreement anywhere about art itself, and under these circumstances we must go back to the beginning, to concern ourselves with dots and circles and lines and all the rest of it. The purposes for which you are acquiring these skills will become apparent, in a superficial way, when you leave school and get a job, but the real meaning of all this is something you will have to find out for yourself, for no one can tell you.

It would be tempting, as I have said, and fashionable as well, to find in this book new evidence that modern life is a spiritual vacuum. But it would be entirely beside the point, for Armin Hofmann is saying something quite different. He is saying, in both words and drawings, that modern life is indeed desperately fragmented, and that this condition is mirrored in education. But rather than deplore these facts, he chooses to accept them, and thus he comes to the view that there has been a "radical alteration in the structure of the applied arts", and that more changes are in the making. By confronting these realities, he thus arrives naturally at the conviction that if problems can be correctly stated, they can be solved.

Curiously enough, in making this confrontation he arrives at a position no different from that of thoughtful people in other disciplines. "We must accustom ourselves", he says, "to the idea that our mental and vocational equipment must be constantly refurbished". The same conclusion is presented by those concerned with the displacement of workers by technical advances. The necessity of "unity" in a world where old guide lines have been erased is a major preoccupation of Hofmann. He flatly rejects the notion that "artistic training is autonomous". He talks of "no separation between spontaneous work with an emotional tone and work directed by the intellect". This is an artist and teacher speaking, but it could be a scientist or a statesman.

Hofmann has quite clearly chosen to assume the responsibilities of citizenship in the new world, but because he is a genuinely humble man and a totally dedicated worker, the significance of his modest book may be overlooked. If his words fail to receive the consideration they deserve, however, it would take the most dull and unperceptive of individuals to miss the extraordinary sensitivity and beauty of the drawings he has made to serve as demonstrations. These lovely illustrations recall to mind that even Bach did not consider the writing of finger exercises below his dignity, and that because he wrote them, they are more than mere exercises. The answers to many of the vexing problems which plague art education and training today might be easier to come by if there were more teachers with the artistic integrity, broad intelligence and deep responsibility of Armin Hofmann.

George Nelson

Generally speaking, too little attention is paid to the problems of art in our schools. What is lacking is a creative focus which would be the source of every new insight into the nature of art and would foster every kind of talent. Activities by which the child itself sets great store in its early years, such as playing, making pictures, modeling and taking things apart, etc., are steadily losing importance in our schools. Whereas in elementary education writing, gymnastics and games, drawing, singing, music and handwork do constitute something of a general approach to the arts as a whole, this group of subjects begins to lose its characteristic features the further the child goes up the educational ladder. Language instruction, capable in itself of imparting creative impulses, is usually bogged down at the level of the "absolutely essential" or, in secondary schools, is channeled primarily towards traditional matter. The history of literature is studied, but the student's own imaginary world and powers of self-expression cannot develop adequately. It is only in drawing, which occupies an isolated and underprivileged position in the curriculum, that thinking, inventing, representing, transposing and abstracting can be correlated. The fact that art activities are not included among school examination subjects is another reason why drawing is rated as merely of secondary importance.

Except for students undergoing a purely artistic training, even the technical colleges and universities provide no courses in which the process of design and original creation is conceded to have any general educational value. The student with creative gifts can hardly develop any further under such unfavorable conditions. Under the present-day system with its emphasis on standard knowledge and the presentation of subject matter, he becomes an outsider.

What reasons can be advanced for this bias in our education? Is it primarily the schools themselves which believe they must adhere to educational subjects that can be conveyed, assessed and stored more readily than activities in which imagination and creative gifts can be given free rein? Or is it that the curricula are influenced from outside by the prevailing trend towards the accumulation of rapidly and easily assimilated knowledge? Whatever the reasons may be for this bias towards the presentation of knowledge, there is no doubt that it fails to provide a basis for fruitful educational work. Questions of composition, combination and variation cannot be dealt with within such a curriculum. The creative student cannot develop and his valuable gifts become stunted.

It is a fairly general assumption that art training is autonomous and subject only to its own laws. It is precisely this error which has induced me to preface my consideration of the problems of art education with some thoughts on education in general with a view to showing the close interdependence of the various aims of education. As a natural consequence of the inadequate art training given during the years of compulsory schooling, the art school is left with a legacy of almost insoluble problems. There are two characteristics which are becoming increasingly prominent among students now entering the preliminary classes of the art school:
1. A fundamentally wrong assessment of the problems facing anyone working in the art field today.
2. A wrong approach to the problems awaiting solution: dashing off a rapid piece of works is all-important, development and painstaking preparation are of no importance at all.

To my mind, these two points make it particularly necessary to reexamine the basis of both preliminary and specialized art training. Superficial handling of pictorial values, which is, of course, partly a consequence of education with no proper basis, must be dealt with firmly at an early stage, particularly where vocations are involved which are closely concerned with the affairs of everyday life. Sound preparatory work with the primary aim of recognizing artistic, creative and technical principles would be impossible if exploitation, taste, fashion and other rapidly changing influences were to be given a place in instruction. This does not mean, of course, that student's exercises should be done in a vacuum and yield nothing that can be evaluated or placed in a context. On the contrary: recognizability and utility must be included from the very start among the aims of the exercise. Here we have the first approach to applied activity. The student who can represent rising, falling, opposed and radiating elements with simple means has taken the initial step towards the application of his art. It would be wrong to conceive the work of the designer as anything but the service of giving messages, events, ideas and values of every kind a visible form. The purpose of the preliminary course is to prepare a well-defined central area from which paths can branch off in everey direction. The profession of graphic designer is only one of these paths. Perhaps today it is one of the most important, but we must not make the mistake of shaping the preliminary course too much to the pattern of this profession, which is the very one constantly subject to the most marked vocational bias and inner change.

Whereas a few years ago the activities of the graphic designer were mainly restricted to the creation of posters, advertisements, packaging, signs, etc., his work has now expanded to embrace virtually every field of representation and design. It is inevitable that this expansion should assume an ever wider scope for reasons which need not be discussed in detail here. One of the most important, however, deserves mention. In recent years industrialization and automation have meant that a number of craftsmen who used to play an important role in the field of applied art have now been deprived of their functions of creation and design or even that the crafts have gone out of existence. There are signs that, besides the lithographer, process engraver and engraver, not to mention the sign-writer, cabinet-maker, art metal-worker, etc., other typical representatives of the applied arts group, such as the compositor and letterpress printer, will also be overtaken by mechanization. The changes within these trades, or even their disappearance, have given rise to a new situation. The creative side of the trades mentioned has now been largely handed over to the designer and the mechanical side increasingly to the machine. This radical alteration in the structure of the applied arts means that the designer of today must combine a knowledge of photography, industrial design, typography, drawing, spatial representation, reproduction techniques, language, etc.

It will be obvious that educators in a field which has been affected by such a revolution must decide afresh where the main accents are to lie. The creation of closer relationships between forces which have hitherto been isolated is a subject which far transcends the bounds of art and may be regarded as one of the great problems of our age. From this point of view the structure of most curricula is inadequate and unsuitable for giving shape to fresh impulses. It is urgent, therefore, that educators should stop thinking in terms of results and thus clear the way for an outlook which embraces a wider field of activities and is more alert to their finer and deeper interrelationships. Line, plane surface, color, material, space and time should be presented to students as a coherent whole. For example, by extending the angle of vision from the two-dimensional surface to the three-dimensional space, quite different pairs of contrasting elements are obtained, and there are many more and much richer possibilities of confrontation than were previously afforded by the plane surface with its contrasts of point–line, thin–thick, circle–square, softened effect–hardness, etc. Adding a new dimension means an extension of the principles of design, not merely in the sense of a numerical increase of existing disciplines, but rather in the sense of completing a constantly expanding unit. Individual values must be investigated in relation to their common denominator. It is necessary that the curriculum should be arranged and the teachers selected so that any one area of subject matter can be reciprocally related to any other. Instead of an extensive accumulation of subjects, a single unit will appear in which the various aspects continually interpenetrate, stimulate and enrich each other. Even apparently remote areas should receive more attention so that starting points may be found for new combinations and fusions of forces.

The problem of reorganizing basic schooling and specialized training in the art vocations clamors for greater attention particularly because of the enormous advances made in industry and technology. The very instruments we have been accustomed to using for expressing ourselves have become mechanized. Pen and pencil, it is true, have remained as our basic implements, but an industry manufacturing mechanical instruments and pencils, crayons, etc., (all with the features of small handy machines) is beginning to influence and confuse the student. A paper industry which sets out to prefabricate every shade of color is going to make color-mixing a thing of the past. A fully developed type-founding industry is changing all our work with lettering. The camera with all its versatility embracing extreme realism, abstraction, movement, color, etc., presupposes a new artistic vision. And in the background there are reproduction processes with laws of their own which are still far from being fully recognized and which, indeed, are constantly infringed as a result of the naive belief that they are purely rational.

The schools are therefore faced with a new task in the sifting, testing and grouping of the instruments and means of representation and production which are constantly appearing on the market. The manufacturers themselves usually give little heed to the new developments they set in motion. Hitherto this problem has been virtually ignored by the schools and the students have been left to select their own instruments. Until recently, for example, each tool for producing graded effects in grey tone (pencil, pen, charcoal, brush, etc.) and each tool for producing color effects (crayon, colored chalk, brush, etc.) was appropriate for the job it had to do and was a natural choice. But now we are suddenly forced to realize that the more mechanical and impersonal nature of the new

implements has challenged the whole basis of our thinking. For instance, we can already dimly see in outline a new style of drawing and designing which has been called into being by ball-point pens, felt nibs, rapidographs, etc.

The school must vigorously oppose the view that, given proper modern technical equipment, one can live in a perfectly functioning organization requiring no personal effort or input, and automatically enjoy success and financial security. The instruments and aids that are placed in our hands nowadays are far too tricky for us to use them unquestioningly. The more cunningly devised they are, the greater the knowledge that is required before they can be put to wise and responsible use.

Instead of accommodating itself to the rapid progress taking place in every field today, the school should, in its own sphere, take the lead in such developments; it must remember its function as a trail-blazer and reorganize itself accordingly. The man of today is chronically short of time. The smaller his store of energy, the less rest he can obtain, the more significant must be the values the creative worker throws into the balance.

The fewer the vocations remaining today that still have a creative contribution to make to a piece of work, the more fully and basically must those educational institutions be equipped where artistic growth can take place. The less experimental work done by people engaged in the actual practice of a profession and intent on extracting from it as much material gain as they can, the more energy and careful thought must the schools devote to experiment and research. This is of particular concern to us because we have hitherto been accustomed to working on subject matter – and even results – supplied to us by practitioners. Now we can see with increasing clarity that it is our business to recognize, plan and stimulate coming trends. This is quite contrary to modern advertising technique which, as a rule, merely exploits situations but does nothing to create new ones. Sales graphs are too uncertain a clue to the course that will be followed by the events ahead.

The problems broached here warrant the following question. How must art teaching today be organized so that it can adapt itself to the latest developments, so that it can bend to its own purposes the technical means now available to it, so that all the varied requirements of design in a highly industrialized world will be recognized and the solutions devised gain general acceptance? It would be rash to believe in simple solutions. But I hold that certain particularly urgent steps can and must be taken today:

1. The line of demarcation between general education, specialized training and continuing education must be drawn in such a way that work can be deepened and diversified on certain themes without a break in continuity and without any final end in view.
2. Schools must be set up for people who have completed their training and are actively pursuing their profession. The times are past when study and training undertaken in youth lasted a whole lifetime. We must accustom ourselves to the idea that our mental and vocational equipment must be constantly refurbished and that our chances of making an effective contribution to an essential process depend on the regularity with which we bring our knowledge up to date.
3. The boundaries between work as practice and work merely aimed at a particular result must be removed. Every exercise or study which is properly done must show a result, and every valid result must have aspects which provide scope for exercise and experiment.
4. No dividing line must be drawn in future between work done with art qualities in view and work done with merely a commercial application in view. A valid form of unity can be found.
5. There should be no separation between spontaneous work with an emotional tone and work directed by the intellect. Both are supplementary to each other and must be regarded as intimately connected. Discipline and freedom are thus to be seen as elements of equal weight, each partaking of the other.

6. The interdependence between design and reproduction must be reconsidered. Today applied art works primarily in the service of industrial mass production. The modernization and rationalization of designing methods, the use of more refined instruments and the introduction of more efficient machines are not in themselves enough to complete the transition from production by craftsmen to production by machines in a satisfactory way. We must realign our whole way of thinking if we are to achieve unity between our creative idea and its realization under the changed circumstances.

Every educator today is faced with the task of preparing young people to work together in building a society based on an honest exchange of labor. Such an aim, however, can be accomplished only in collaboration with the world of practical activity. Neither educators whose minds are turned inwards nor practitioners who exploit for their own private ends the resources and power provided by research for the general good can form a basis on which an authentic culture appropriate to our age can grow. Collaboration between educators and practitioners is thus something that goes to the roots of our existence.

Armin Hofmann

The idea of a dot must be understood in a very broad sense. All plane figures which have a center and are perceived as closed forms may be described as being dot-shaped. And even if a dot expands, it still remains a dot. A mere increase in the size of an element is not enough to alter its essential character. We must be able to recognize an element as such in spite of the accidentals of a particular embodiment. The dot may grow large and cover a flat area; in which case the question arises as to its precise external form, its color value and its surface texture. But when it is found in its smallest form, all these questions are superfluous.

Because it is circumscribed, balanced, non-figurative and weightless, the smallest dot is particularly well adapted to demonstrating the most important principles of composition. It is the most maneuverable element in the whole field of pictorial art – it is really a building block of instruction.

It is also rewarding from the technical point of view to look into the mobility of the dot. When any pictorial work is transferred to a printing surface, it is the dot alone that can make graded tone values, colors, transitions and blends reproducible. The whole technique of graphic reproduction is based on the small unit of the dot.

Exercises with dots – the most important graphic element – are particularly instructive when performed in the medium of lithography. Especially in our day when for the first time design is developing along separate lines from printing techniques, a great deal can be learned from the close artistic and technical relationship which is possible between the original and the reproduction in lithography.

If we place the smallest dot in the center of a square, its forces begin to make themselves felt at once. The two values dot–background must, however, always be proportioned to each other, otherwise too large a dot disrupts too small a background or too large a background overwhelms too small a dot.

In the safe middle ranges the dot readily establishes contact with its environment. The problem assumes a particular interesting form in marginal situations. At what moment does the dot emerge as such from its environment? Are there already relationships at this early stage of its appearance? It takes considerable artistic discernment to seek out and fix the extreme limits of a consonance between two elements. Throughout the region of marginal consonances there are great possibilities of producing tensions. The most marked tensions arise in the neighbourhood of disturbing forces, in the zone where there is a danger of one element being engulfed or overpowered by another.

Every dot, even the smallest, has radiating power; it is most at home in the center of its environment. But the dot– plane relationships invariably proceed exclusively outwards from the dot or inwards towards it. There is something unconditional and final about a dot in the center. In practical applications, it is true, the radiating power of the absolute center is of extreme importance, but a freer play of forces is needed to create more vital relationships. If the dot is displaced from the center, the static relationship between dot and background is unsettled. Above all, the somewhat passive plane of the background now becomes aggressive. It succeeds in startling the dot into flight, driving it round or forcing it to the outer limits. The illusion of space might even be evoked.

If we place another dot by the side of the first one, the dot-background relationship, which was previously the only contact, now becomes secondary. The two dots determine what happens on the plane. Their forces are reciprocally engaged along a linear path. When appropriately arranged, they can cut the plane into two parts and break out of the format. If we shorten the distance between the dots so that they impinge on each other, we have a pair of dots out of which the most varied new dot structures develop as the degree of fusion between them increases. In a triangle of dots this reciprocal action along the

lines between the dots creates a stream of
forces which is closed within itself;
the movements remain within the format.
Working with a large number of dots
gives a rich variety of formulations:
simple rows of dots, vertical and
horizontal rows of dots (grid pattern),
grouping, free and selective scattering,
massing, variability in size, grey tone and
color, and in texture.

Just as the expansion of the dot into a
plane surface does not affect its nature,
so the spatial expansion of the dot
into a sphere leaves its essential character
untouched. Through the addition of an
extra dimension, the sphere simply gives
added weight to the statement. The
radiating power of the sphere is greater
than that of the disc; through the
addition of the new dimension, the
pattern of forces has increased and the
center must intensify its activity. Just
as with the smallest dot, so in the case
of the smallest sphere, for example, a
speck of dust, the question of its
characteristics does not arise, yet,
hard though it is to visualize, these
continue to exercise their effect.

In this book particular attention is
paid to the combination of plane surfaces
and three-dimensional elements. The
reasons are twofold: first, to keep
track of fundamental forces and, second,
to enable us to make the transition
from two-dimensional to three-
dimensional designing in entirely concrete
terms. We must endeavour to do away
with artificially imposed limits which have
now lost their validity.

In our exercises with dots the line figured repeatedly in the important role of a connecting link. In one case this connection between two distant dots is invisible – it is simply imagined; in another case where dots follow very closely upon one another in a linear arrangement, it already appears as an independent force. If one runs a pencil over a paper, a line appears which is made up of dots so small that they can no longer be recognized as such. Only by using suitable instruments, particularly the brush and drawing pen, can a compact line be produced with a fluid medium. But even in this case it should be remembered that the line is the visible trace of a moving dot. Hence the line is dependent on the dot; it presupposes the dot as its own basic element.

Movement is the real domain of the line. Unlike the dot, which is bound to a center and is therefore static, the line is dynamic by nature. It can be continued indefinitely in either direction, it is bound neither to a form nor to a center. If the line is nevertheless conceived as a basic element, this is only because the process that created it is no longer perceptible as such. The line is an element that has already gone through a process of growth.

If the dot is an important element in structure and analysis, the line performs the important duty of construction. It joins, articulates, bears, supports, holds together and protects; lines intersect and ramify.

The simplest configuration of lines is the grid of vertical or horizontal lines. If a thin line is repeated at constant intervals it produces a solid grey effect in which the single line is no longer discernible, analogous to the way in which the individual dot merges its separate existence into that of a uniform mass of dots.

If we remove individual lines from the grid, new ones instantly appear – but on a different plane. This makes us realize that two qualities of essentially equal value are operative in the grid: namely the black line and the white line, which are at all times interdependent. Two straight parallel lines produce a third enclosed between them. The relationship of negative–positive, one of the most important encounters between opposites in all design work, arises automatically. The space in between, which is a by-product, is just as important as the element producing it.

Progressively increasing the distance between the lines, slowly thickening the line itself, taking away from above or below, slanting the line within the field of operations – all these are processes which, because of their very simplicity, recall fundamental but forgotten knowledge to our minds.

Like the dot, the line does not change its nature, however extended it becomes. But unlike the dot, which, however much enlarged, still appears to the eye as a dot, the line, when extended, rapidly passes from the field of vision. If the line is thickened too much in proportion to its length, the eye sees it as a plane surface. The line as such can only be mentally grasped in terms of the relationship between its length and width. It is more easily affected by distance than the dot.

The thin line, like the small dot, is not a suitable vehicle for color. Even if infinitely prolonged, it is difficult for it to give tone and color values any scope for display. If its thickness is increased enough for color to have an adequate field of action, then, to remain a line, its length must be extended beyond visual range. The black line loses its intensity and turns grey as it gets thinner. The white line holds out longest against a black background. It gains additional luminosity as it grows thinner.

In the field of reproduction the woodcut, the linocut and the etching are particularly suitable for linear designs because in these original techniques both the material and the instruments lend themselves ideally to the production of line. In the woodcut and the linocut the line cut in the material appears negative (white on black) in the print. For a black line on a white ground a more complicated process is necessary. The etching genuinely produces a positive black line on a white ground, although, to the superficial observer, the actual operation, the formation of the line, seems basically the same as that in the woodcut and the linocut. The etching is better suited than almost any other medium for making lines of extreme delicacy. The ungrained smooth lithographic stone, the offset plate and, more recently, the film, offer the least resistance to the production of line. Linear designs can be easily drawn with a pen or brush. The material itself sets no limits to refinements in the thickness of the stroke or to the rapidity with which the strokes can be executed.

All these methods of reproduction have been rendered obsolete by the latest technical developments. All the same, they do afford the students today a practical opportunity of coming to grips with basic methods within the field of reproduction where processes are growing constantly more complicated. In these primary printing techniques trimmings and frills must be dispensed with. The purest expression of line, the manifestation of its essence so to say, is invariably attained with the most success when – like every other pictorial element – it is conceived with its reproduction by a printing technique in mind.

Encounters between dissimilar elements within compositions containing dots or lines only can be readily followed even if complicated arrangements and formations are involved. In compositions depending on contrasts, such as much–little, horizontal–vertical, dynamic–static, light–dark, etc., the basic idea can be deciphered without difficulty. But the creation of consonances, in which the individual elements are taken from worlds of mutually alien character and in which movements and groupings always follow their own laws, confronts the student with complicated and unfamiliar processes. To bring together in harmony two disparate systems necessarily presupposes a greater depth of artistic perception and the courage to embark upon new trains of thought and novel formulations.

Even in the early stages, bringing together two opposed components proves to be extremely fruitful because, as the basis of more complicated composition studies, it already affords new insights of decisive importance. The meeting of a square and a circle within a predetermined field of action has been selected as the basic example in the following chapter. Confrontation is a theme on which variations can be played with any desired consonances, with any imaginable values and in a great variety of ways. Hence a number of examples which strictly belong to the chapter on confrontation will be found scattered all over the book. To bring together disparate values, to achieve equilibriums of every kind, to resolve opposites on a higher plane is a task transcending the problems considered here from the graphic point of view and has, indeed, become one of the cardinal tasks of our age.

Combining design and lettering epitomizes the special world of harmonics in which the graphic designer works. The difficult task of unifying two different kinds of graphic systems is characteristic of his vocation and is also a clue to what is required in his training. This basic dyad is of an unusual character; its complexity becomes apparent only when the two systems involved are carefully studied.

Writing is purely a means of communication built up from linear geometrical signs which are understood on the basis of mutual agreement. But the system had first to be invented and it requires a mental effort on everybody's part to elicit a message from signs which were hitherto unfamiliar. The picture, on the other hand, contains an inherent message. Although it also costs us an effort – and today more than ever before – to "read" its outward forms, which may range from a realistic depiction or a stylized representation to a non-figurative picture, it nevertheless speaks to us directly. Unlike lettering, the picture radiates movements, tone values and forms as forces which evoke an immediate response. The reconciliation of this typical antagonism calls for a great deal of knowledge and skill in all tasks where picture and lettering are to be combined.

In applied art the problem must always be solved with the technique of reproduction in mind. In the case of the woodcut, the etching and the lithography, the nature of the instrument and the printing surface inevitably led to the picture and lettering being conceived in the same spirit and executed in a manner appropriate to the material. As soon as the movable letter was introduced in letterpress printing, lettering began to develop in its own way, with the result that, with industrialization, the process of lettering was partitioned off and became extremely complicated technically. Similarly the versatility of modern printing methods, the advent of photography and motion pictures and, last but not least, the new formal language of painting have invested the picture with great expressive power, but at the same time they have made the initial conditions for producing a picture substantially more difficult. Today it is a practical impossibility to acquire a mastery of every separate technical and artistic aspect of the creation of pictures and lettering. There has been a change in the functions of the graphic designer. Today he must know, on the one hand, precisely what can be offered him by the highly specialized branches into which the originally simple and readily understood printing trade has split and, on the other hand, he must develop and realign his artistic perception accordingly. Only then will he be able to find creative solutions to the problems presented by a confrontation of opposites.

Probably very few people are conscious of the structure of our letter system. These legible symbols are too familiar to provoke us into reflections on their basic construction. Perhaps it should be emphasized that we resort to the basic elements of creative art when we compose or receive a written message. From this point of view, letter forms assume considerable importance in that, apart from their actual function as a means of communication, they also afford one of the few occasions when modern man has to deal with the pure formal element. This means an increased responsibility for those who work with lettering and letter forms in an influential capacity.

In the training of graphic designers a considerable part of the curriculum is taken up by writing letters in imitation of historical models, drawing letters, constructing and composing letters and, to an increasing extent, by the composition of printing type. Work on lettering is certainly the part of their training which is most clearly marked out in advance because of the stability of the traditional forms and the traditional system; but this tradition-bound atmosphere is also the least susceptible to the winds of change.

Previously, the way to teach lettering was clearly defined, for the work to be done in actual practice formed the basis for the course of instruction. Accordingly the work revolved largely round the shaping of individual letters, creating new types of letters and ornamental and fancy letters. Lithography, which was for a long time the main means of reproduction, was well-adapted for hand-drawn letters in every respect. But now, when graphic reproduction has been revolutionized by the mechanization of almost all its processes, the designer is precluded from having any direct influence on the future development of letters. The hand-drawn word and the logotype designed specially for a specific purpose have become rare.

People working with letters today find that their task consists increasingly of the combination of ready-made components. As the development of letters in the next few years is bound to be determined by the important type-founders, we know roughly what lines this further development is likely to take: above all it will be characterized by a more and more pronounced gradation within the familiar series of type faces. The designer will be in the position of a composer who can produce ever richer sound patterns because of the ever more finely differentiated categories of type faces at his disposal. It is this maneuverability with varieties of type displaying richer and finer shades of distinction which must guide us in the organization of future courses in lettering.

The designing of whole alphabets and the study of historical letter forms remain indispensable to the teaching of form. At the same time, however, new paths must be explored so that a sense of the finest distinctions can be cultivated, so that the basic elements of our letters can appear in a new form, and so that those special abilities for combining are developed which lettering will demand in future. The creation of all those symbols and logotypes which are an ever more striking feature of the world in which we live calls for a new and fresh approach to lettering on the part of the designer. In these logotypes the combination of letters can be more or less obvious; but only deliberately contrived encounters of elements and confrontations of values can lead beyond the letters to new forms of expression.

The dot

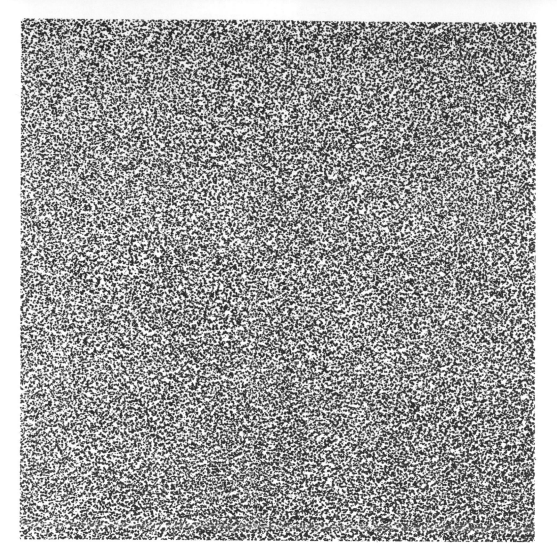

1

**1**
The dot is produced when a pencil or crayon is passed over a roughly grained surface. (Lithograph)
**2**
The dot ist produced by briefly touching a smouth surface with pen and India ink.

2

22

A combination of two different processes. The small white dots are produced indirectly by chalking over the roughly grained surface, whereas the white dot in the center is cut out with a sharp instrument, such as a scraper. (Lithograph)

3

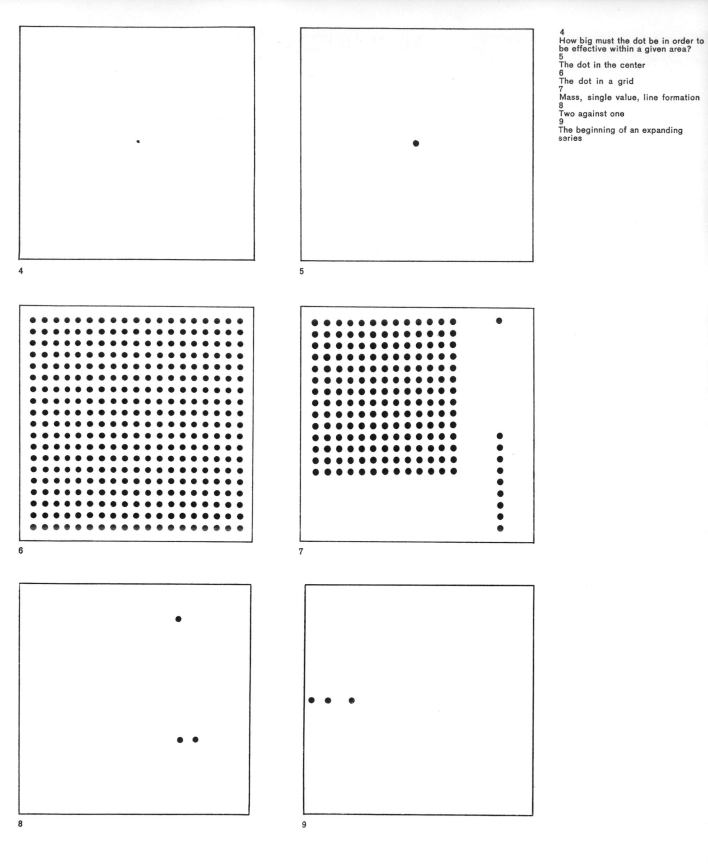

4
How big must the dot be in order to
be effective within a given area?
5
The dot in the center
6
The dot in a grid
7
Mass, single value, line formation
8
Two against one
9
The beginning of an expanding
series

4

5

6

7

8

9

24

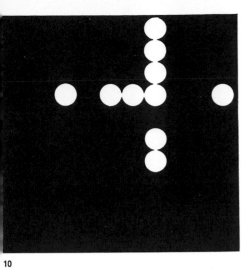

10

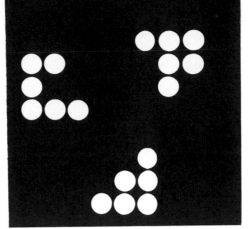

11

10
Cross of dots separated out from
the grid pattern
11
Three groups of dots from the same
pattern
12
Free distribution without a grid
pattern

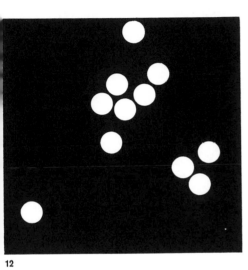

12

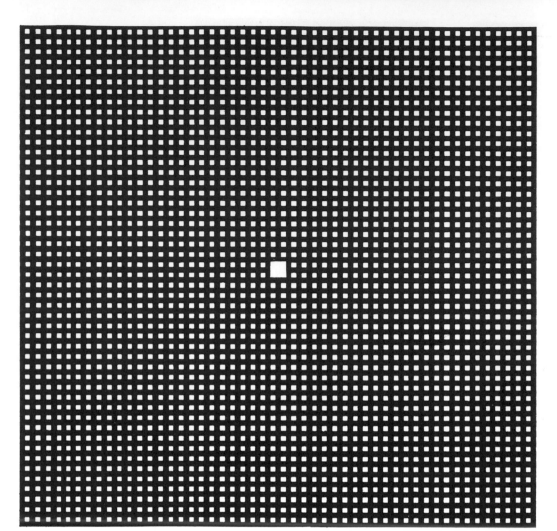

13
The square dot. The lattice grid
automatically produces square dots.
Only deliberate interference with
the grid makes the gap stand out as
a dot. The situation is similar to
No. 3.

If the lines of the lattice grid are interrupted, the white dots combine to form symbols and figures.

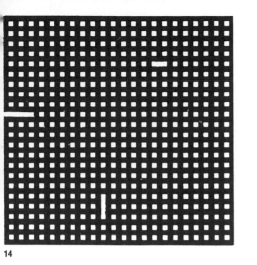

14

15

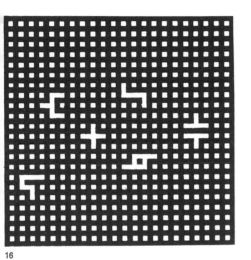

16

17

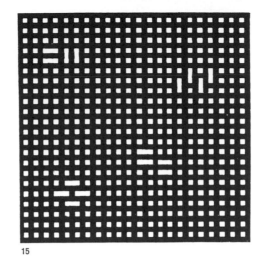

18

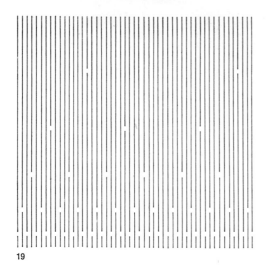

19

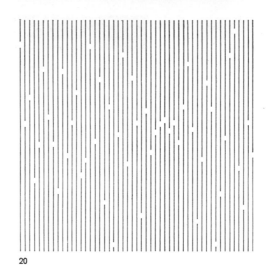

20

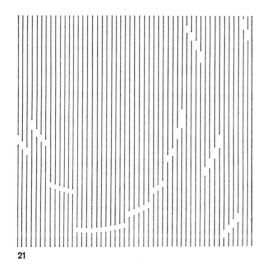

21

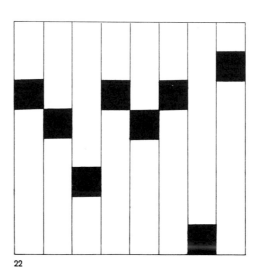

22

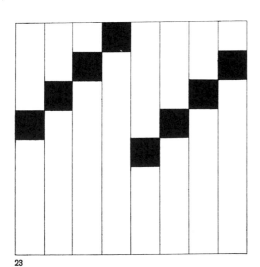

23

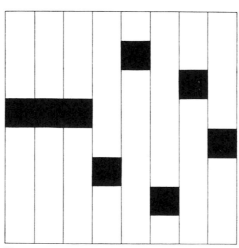

24

**19 20 21**
If the lines in a grid of thin lines are interrupted, the dot is produced by the gap and the interstitial spaces at its sides. These dots can once again combine to create figures and paths of movement. See No. 73–76.
**22 23 24**
Various patterns of dots separated out from a coarse grid

28

25

26

27 28
Black dots on a white background.
White dots on a black background.
29
Composition study

27

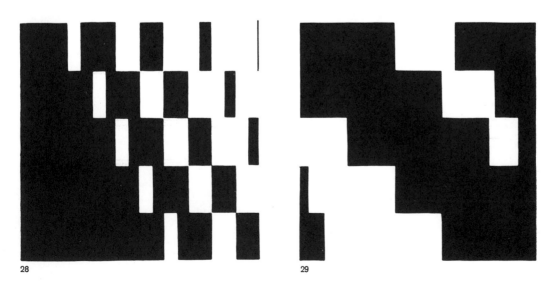

28                                          29

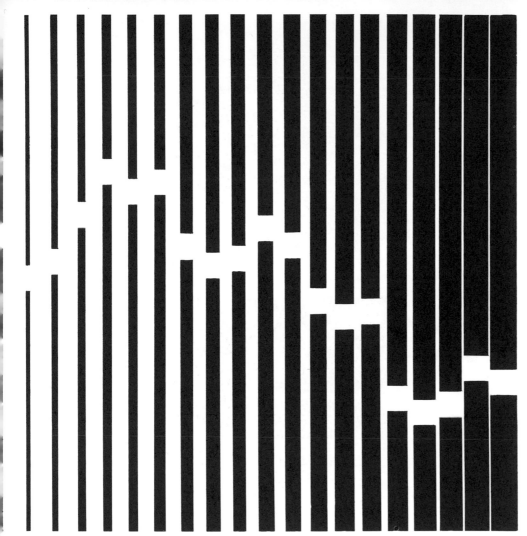

30  31
Same exercise as No. 19–21 but with
progressively thicker lines

0

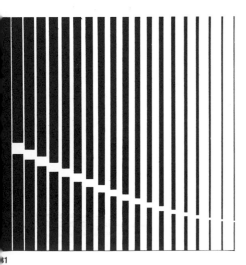

31

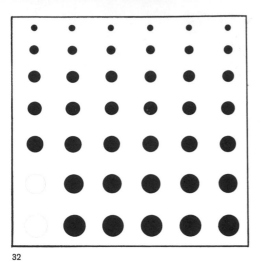

32

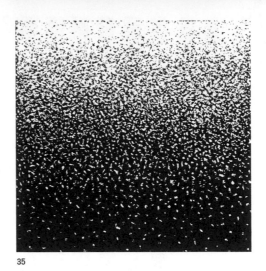

35

32 33 34
The smallest perceptible dot looks round. How big must it be before th question of its shape arises?
35
The slow transition from positive to negative dots is a natural consequence of a chalk stroke.
36
Experiment for a "Winter Aid" poste

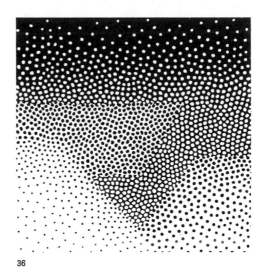

36

33

34

37

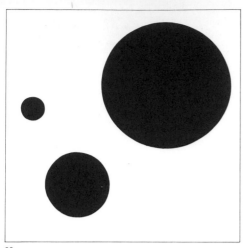

38

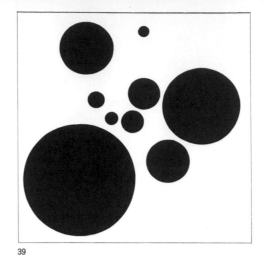

39

40

38
Dots, three sizes
39
Smallest dot isolated
40
Interaction between various groups
of dots
41
Transposition exercise from nature.
Dot formation in an autumn leaf.
(Lithograph, multi-colored, dots
reddish, leaf surface green; contrast
of quantity)

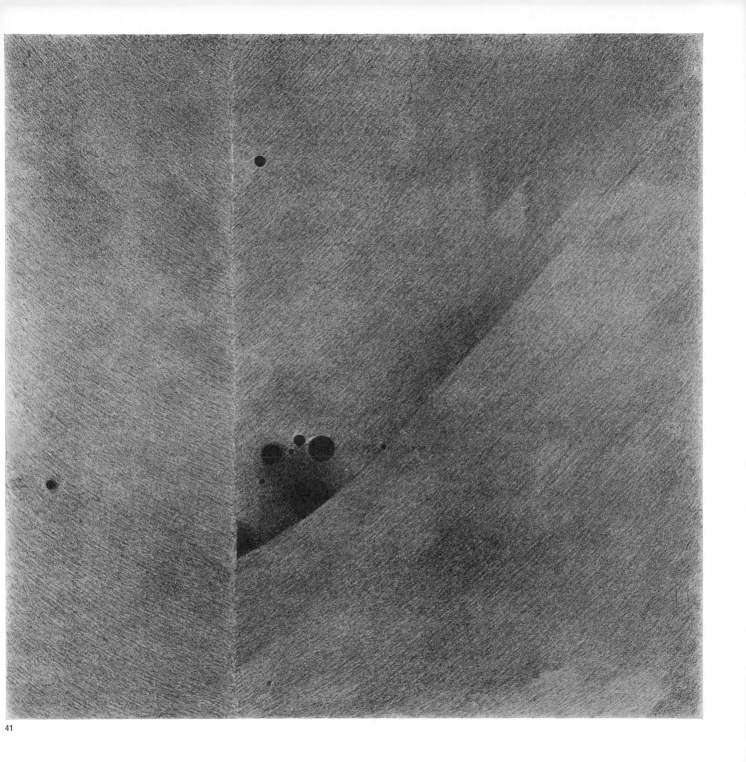

41

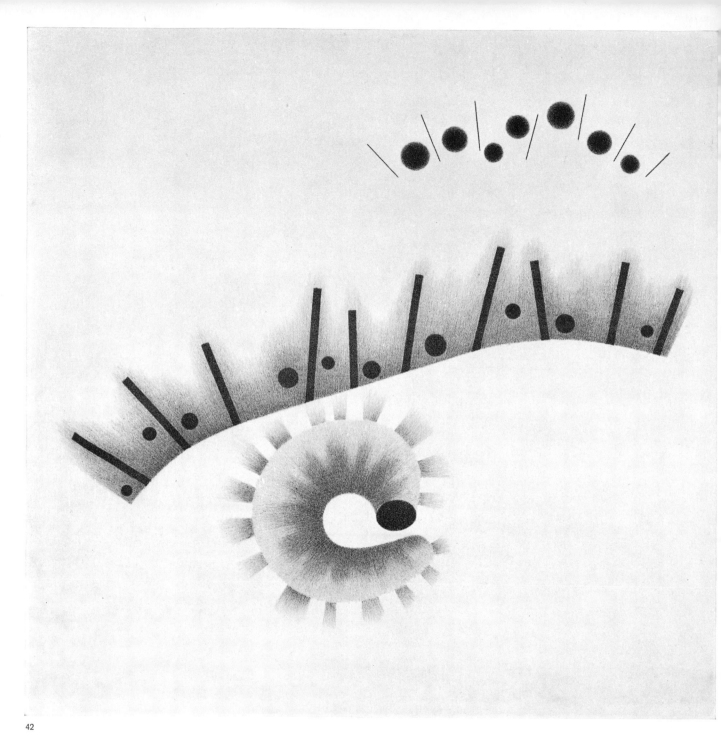

42

42
Transposition exercise from
nature combined with a composition
problem  (Lithograph)
43
Package for caterpillar exterminator.
The dots remain an inherent part of
the composition even when the wrap
is given a three-dimensional form.

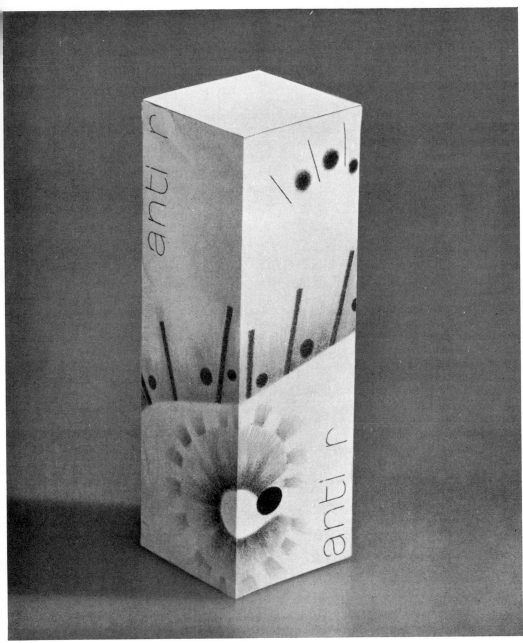

43

44

44
The difference in the size of the dots is now underlined by different values of grey. The basis of the composition is similar to No. 38.
45
Color is now added to the play of light and shade in the different values of grey. A different configuration appears on each side of the package. The interplay between all the visible sides brings in a new compositional element. At the same time the spatial laws of the cube receive due attention.
No. 44 and 45 are preliminary steps leading to spatial compositions with objects in which tone values also play their part.
46
Movements of dots and tone value in objects. The light and dark dots form the background of the composition.
(Executed in collaboration with the photography course)

45

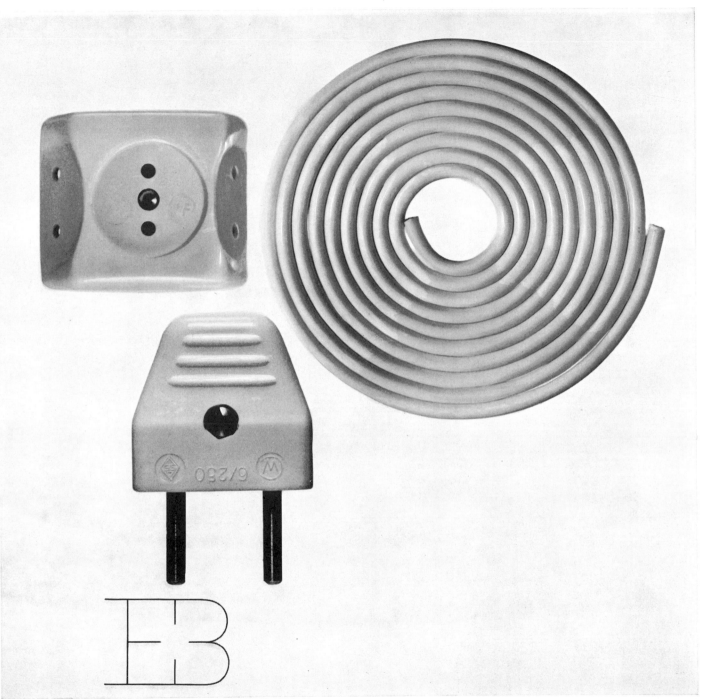

46

The round dot is divided into nine
parts. By blanking out single parts,
figures are obtained which more or
less suggest the basic form.
48
Starting point for the exercise
No. 47

47

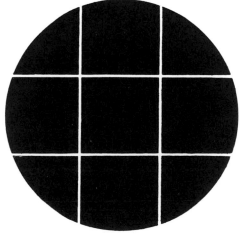

48

Transposition exercise from nature
50
Similar exercise to No. 47. A quarter
of the dot is blanked out, the
remaining figures are turned and
fitted together to make a symbol.

49

50

41

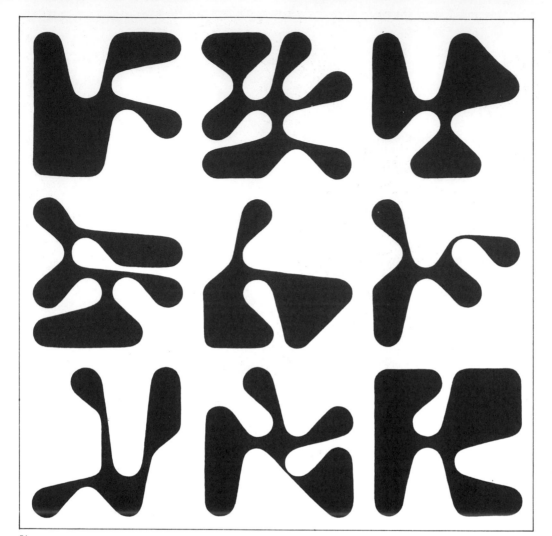

51

51
Study in variations: growing, fluid
structures meet one another.
Starting position: sixteen dots.
Certain dots are singled out and
linked together. The nine variations
thus created are recombined into
a new unit.
52
Starting position for No. 51, figure
53
Transposition exercise from nature.
Dot formation on an autumn leaf.
(Lithograph)

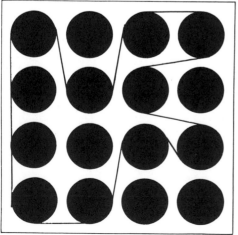

52

54

54
Transposition exercise from pebbles.
Previously the round dot has been
the starting point for the exercises.
But even when the dot is grossly
distorted, it still retains the radiating
power which is inherent in every
dot-shaped structure. This exercise
is basically a variant of composition
study No. 38. (Linocut)
55
Pouring out and flowing away.
Transposition of the process into a
practical exercise.

55

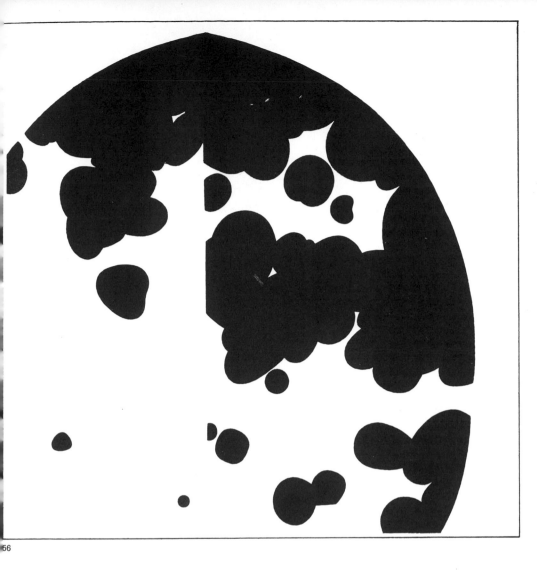

Linked dots in an autumn leaf study
(Lithograph)

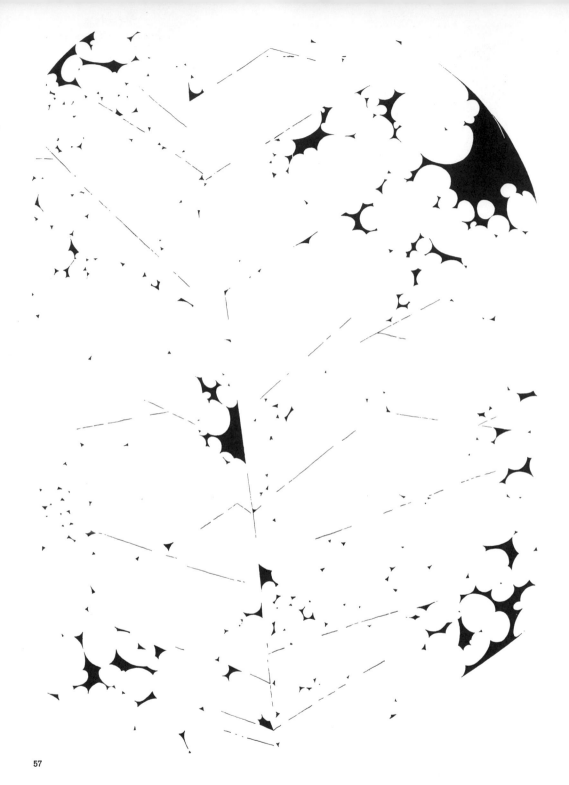

Autumn leaf study. The dots are
intensively massed together and
leave over new and minute dot-
shaped forms. (Lithograph)
58
Container for a plant insecticide.
Whereas in No. 43 and 44 we saw
how groups of dots were disposed
over cubes, here the solid chosen
is the cylinder.

57

Herba force
Pflanzenschutz-
mittel
gegen
Mehltau
Blattläuse
und Käferfrass
500gr Fr. 8.50

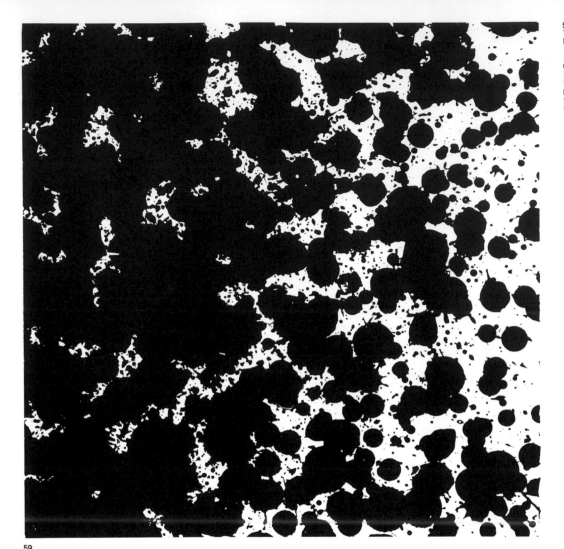

59

59
Traces left by drops, produced
by successive manipulations with
different kinds of brushes
(Lithograph)
60
If we let drops of India ink drip
from a brush onto the paper, the
power inherent in the process is
expressed with particular vividness
in the result obtained: the radiation
bursts forth with explosive power.

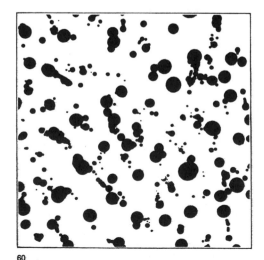

60

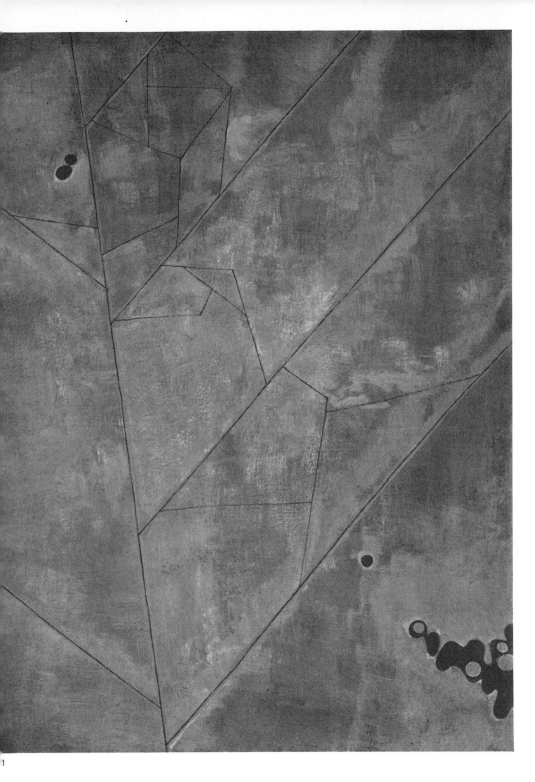

Autumn leaf study. The group of
dots brings its influence to bear on
the line system. (Tempera, multi-
colored: violet-brown dots on an
olive background)

1

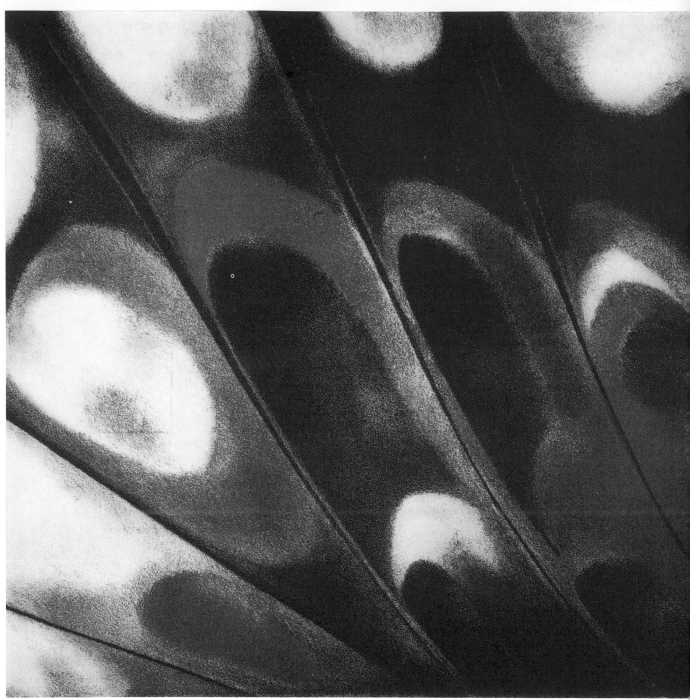

62

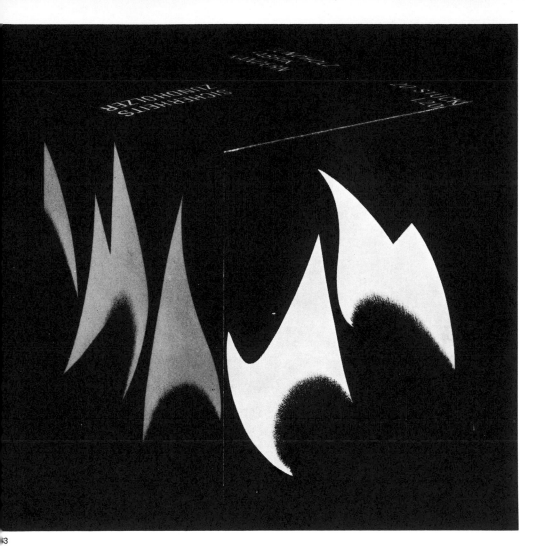

62
Part of a butterfly's wing. The dot is set in motion. (5-color chalk lithograph)
63
Design for a candle box. Situation similar to No. 62. The dots take flight as the candles flare up. (Combination of crayon texture, surface and lettering, drawn on offset plate)
64
Streaming motion of dots, produced by a crayon moved under pressure (Lithograph)

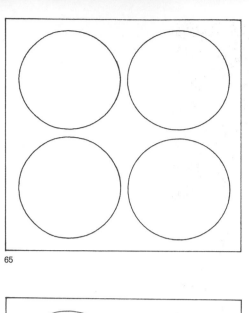

65

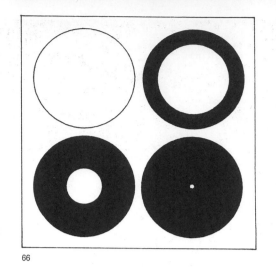

66

65 66 67 68 69
The circle. Exercises similar to
No. 38, 39, 40. In No. 66, 68, 69
variations in size are accompanied
by differences in the thickness of
the line. This gives rise to a new
element: the white dot in the black
dot.

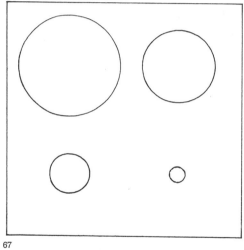

67

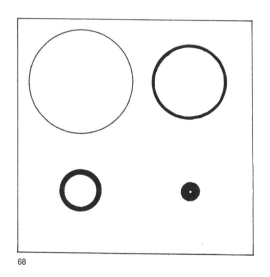

68

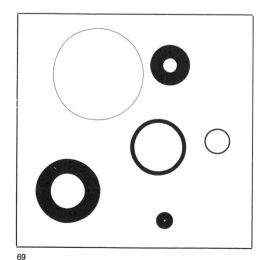

69

52

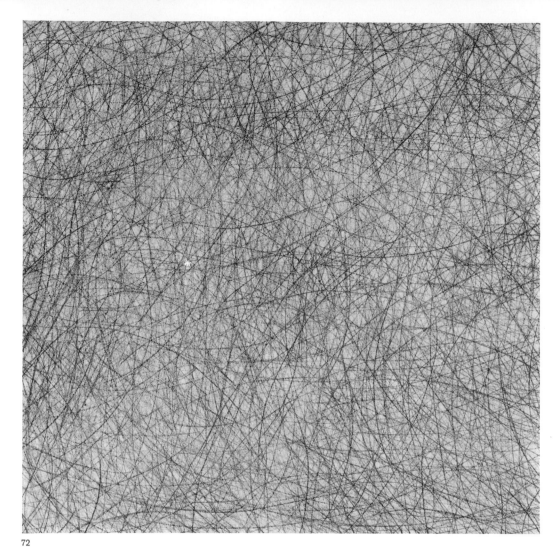

72

73

72
Free exercise with segments of
circles  (Lithograph)
73  74  75  76
The starting point for these exercise
is a circular grid. The various
patterns are obtained by blanking
out different parts of the grid. The
results elicit a wide variety of
sensations: rotating, moving, flitting
past, rocking, crossing, etc. (Exercises executed with a pair of
compasses)

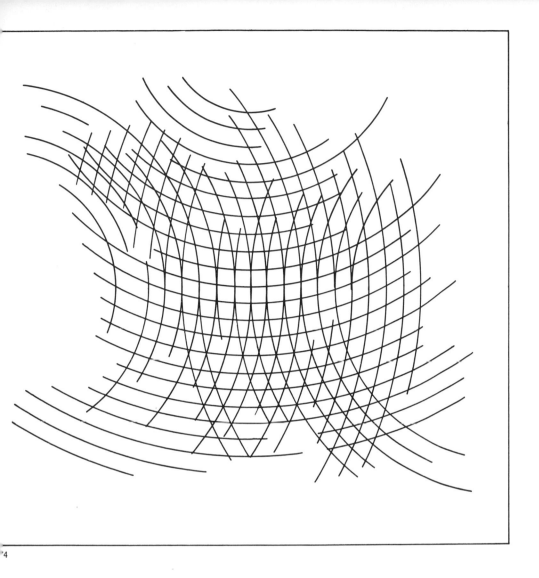

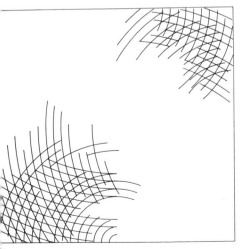

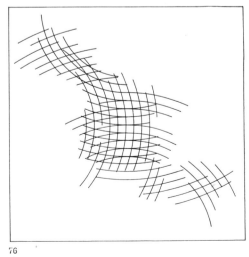

77

78

27 Aug 16 Sept
Mustermesse Halle 9
KINDER täglich
VERKEHRS 14-17 Uhr
GARTEN

79

80
Study in rotation. Particles are
propelled from the central point
along spiral paths. (Lithograph)
81
Study in rotation. Rotary lines are
made direct with a crayon.
(Lithograph)

80

81

Mustermesse
Halle 9
26. Aug.-15. Sept.
14-17 Uhr
Täglich geöffnet
Sonntags
geschlossen

82
Poster for children's traffic school.
The rotating process is initiated
by the lettering. (The letters were
arranged on a gramophone record,
set in motion and then photographed.)

82

83  84  85  86  87  88
The sphere as a space-occupying dot
(Various forms of lighting)

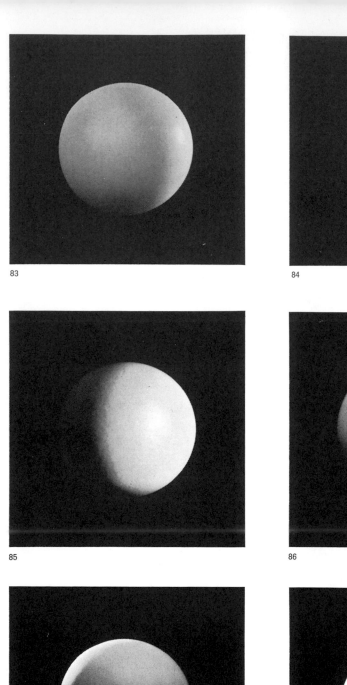

83

84

85

86

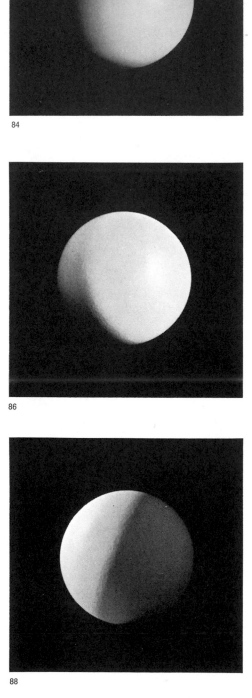

87

88

60

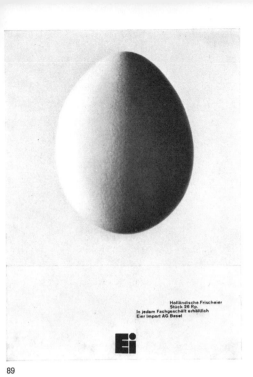

Holländische Frischeier
Stück 26 Rp.
In jedem Fachgeschäft erhältlich
Eier Import AG Basel

89

Holländische Frischeier
Stück 26 Rp.
In jedem Fachgeschäft erhältlich
Eier Import AG Basel

90

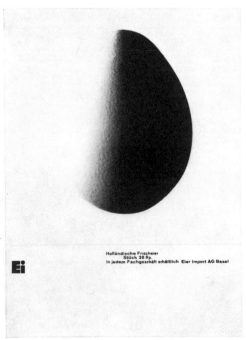

Holländische Frischeier
Stück 26 Rp.
In jedem Fachgeschäft erhältlich Eier Import AG Basel

91

92
Segment of a wooden sphere
93
Composition study with wooden
spheres: large–small, complete–
incomplete, distinct–indistinct,
light–dark.

92

93

Winter hilfe 60

94

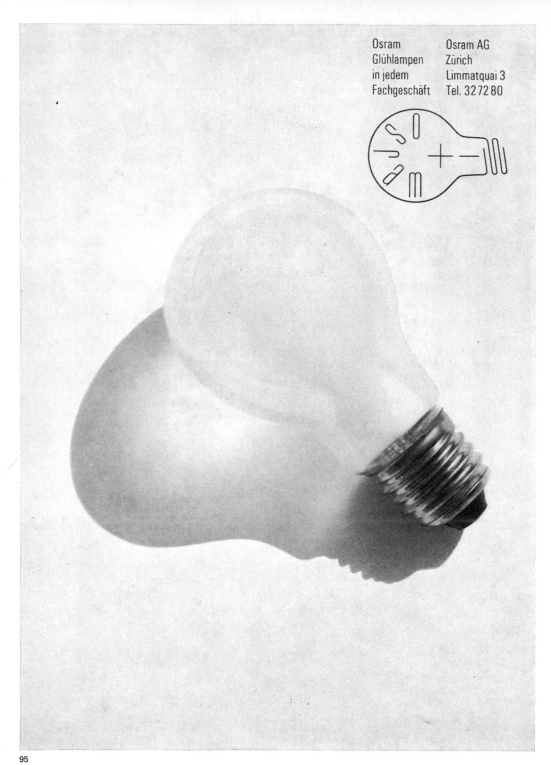

Osram
Glühlampen
in jedem
Fachgeschäft

Osram AG
Zürich
Limmatquai 3
Tel. 32 72 80

95
Advertisement for electric light
bulbs. The daylight shines through
the transparent sphere.

95

Osram
Glühlampen
in jedem
Fachgeschäft
Osram AG
Zürich
Limmatquai 3
Tel. 32 72 80

96
Advertisement for electric light
bulbs. The sphere radiates artificial
light.

97
The object loses its outline and
retreats into the distance because
the blurred setting of the lens.

97

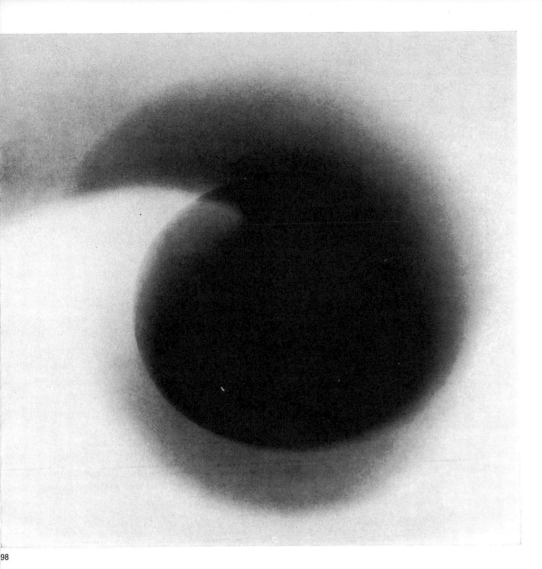

98
First stage of a film poster. The
sphere loses its outline when it is
set in motion. Two associations are
elicited: the human eye, a reel of
film.

98

99

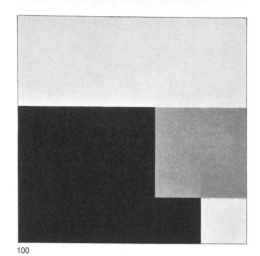

100

99 100 101 102 103
Compositions with dots of different sizes and tone values. These give rise to the most varied associations, such as inclusion and exclusion, standing together, standing side by side, intermeshing, clustering, piling up, sliding to and fro, incorporation of background, separation of background, etc.

101

102

103

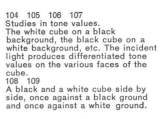

104 105 106 107
Studies in tone values.
The white cube on a black
background, the black cube on a
white background, etc. The incident
light produces differentiated tone
values on the various faces of the
cube.
108 109
A black and a white cube side by
side, once against a black ground
and once against a white ground.

04

105

06

107

108

109

110

110
Arrangement of wooden cubes with
distinct and indistinct outlines.
The increasing indistinctness toward
the rear produces a strong illusion
of space.

No. 83—98 and No. 104—110 were
executed in collaboration with the
photography course.

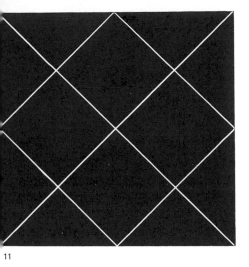

111
Starting point for No. 112 and
No. 113
112
Blanking out some of the parts gives
rise to various plane figures.
113
Water collector at the General Trade
School in Basle. Instead of a pattern
of planes, here the components
form corresponding projections into
space.

11

112

113

114

115
Competition for an inn sign "The Crooked Corner" (Cast concrete)

No. 114 and 115 were executed in collaboration with the course for spatial design.

115

The line

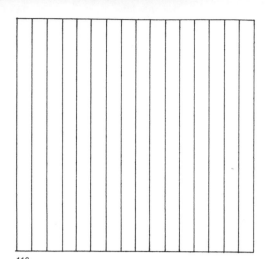

116

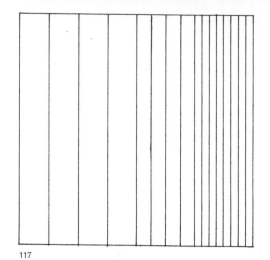

117

116
Uniform repetition of a vertical line
117
Repetition of a vertical line in which the distance between the lines is reduced three times
118
Repetition of thin and thick lines at regular intervals

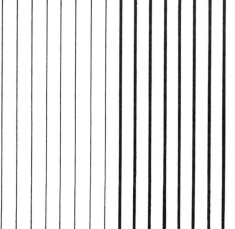

118

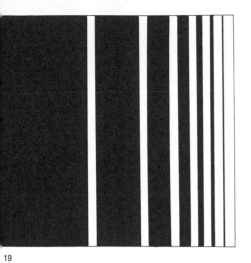

19

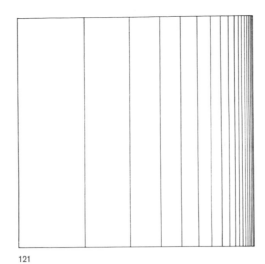

121

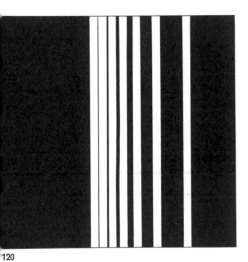

120

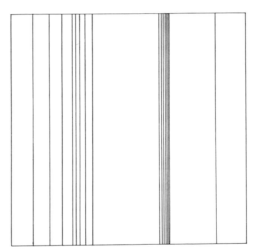

122

119
Progressively widening distances
between regular white strips on a
black background. The white strips
activate the black interspaces.
In contrast to No. 120, the entire
black background is affected by the
rhythm.
120
The gradation begins after the first
third of the background. In this way
the disengaged black third acquires
a quality of its own.
121
Progressively narrowing distances
of lines. The white background
is not affected by the
gradation.
122
Differently graded bundles of
thin lines

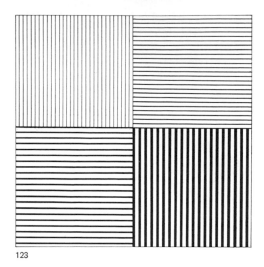

123

123
Study in tone value
124  125  126
Experiments with playing card figures
on the basis of the preceding
exercises

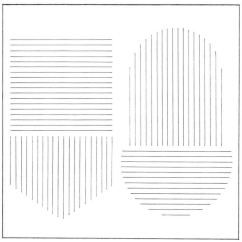

124

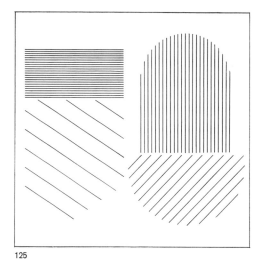

125

126

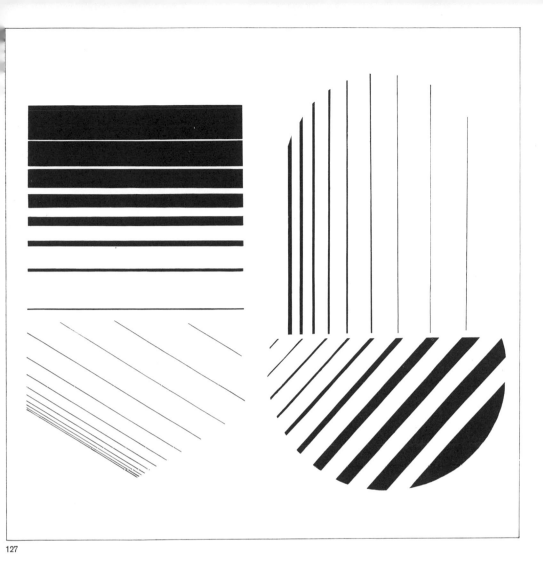

Playing card figures. A particularly
impressive feature here is the
interplay between the primacy of
the black or white lines. In spite of
the lively sense of motion which the
play of lines imparts, it remains
primarily a substitute for tone value.

127

128
Another example of graded tones of
grey produced by different qualites
of lines (Linocut)

128

schrauben
aller
art
metalle
eisen-
und
stahl-
waren
kugellager
depot:
poldi-
stahl

129
Advertisement for hardware manufacturer. The introduction of the
lattice grid evokes the illusion of a
screw-thread. The grey tone thus
produced creates a link with the
group of letters.
130
Advertisement for hardware manufacturer. The lines representing the
screw-thread retain their own value
because of the breadth of the black
intervals. Contrast with group of
letters.
131
Advertisement for hardware manufacturer. Differently graded linear
values.
132
Symbol for hardware manufacturer.
The line performs two kinds of
function at the same time: it forms
the lettering and represents the
object.

129

130

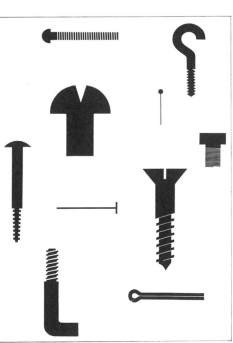

131

132

First stage of a traffic poster. The use of a progressively graded lin[e] evokes the impression of movement and speed. The regular pattern of horizontal lines provides the background against which the general movement takes place.

133

134
Railway poster. What has been learnt in the preceding exercises has been applied here in more elaborate forms. (Line drawing)

135

135 136 137
The illusion of movement previously evoked by a gradation of line thicknesses and interspaces can also be produced by using different tone values.

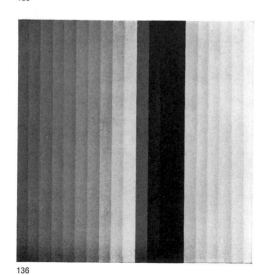

136

137

138

If, in addition to graded tone values, the background is also sectioned on similar lines to No. 119, 120, 122, then a greatly extended range of possible means of expression is obtained.

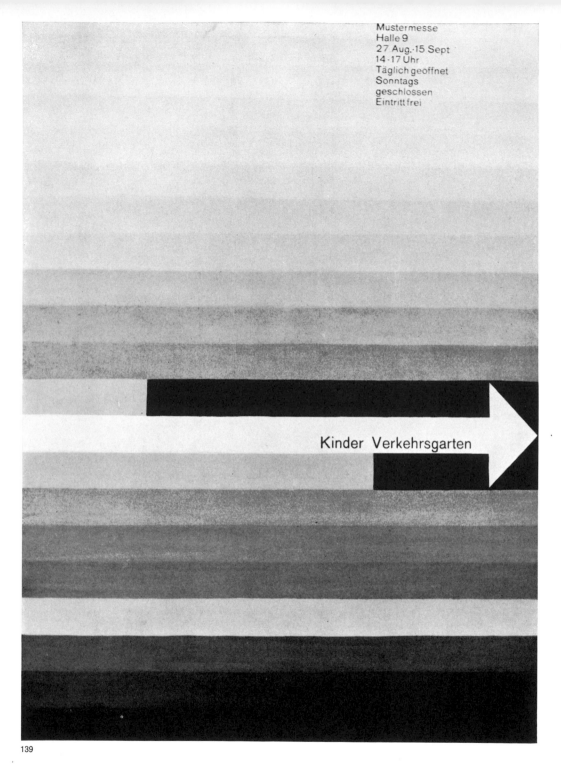

Mustermesse
Halle 9
27 Aug.-15 Sept
14-17 Uhr
Täglich geoffnet
Sonntags
geschlossen
Eintritt frei

Kinder Verkehrsgarten

139
Poster for a children's traffic school.
An arrow penetrates into the scale
of tone values.

139

140
Advertisement for an electric light
bulb manufacturer. Vertical white
values stream into the horizontal
dark areas.

140

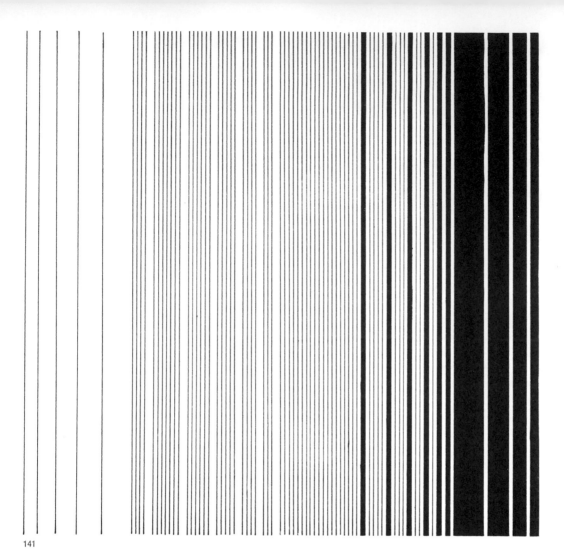

141

141
A suitable arrangement of lines can produce the finest shades of grey which are very close to a solid grey tone.

88

142

142
Relief with the letter i. Incident
light from the left gives rise to lines
with various tone values.
143
The same object with light falling
from the right

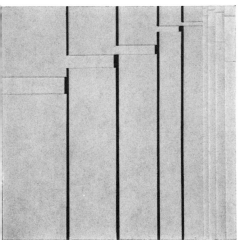

143

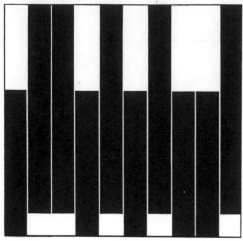

144

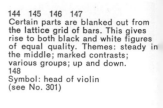
144 145 146 147
Certain parts are blanked out from the lattice grid of bars. This gives rise to both black and white figures of equal quality. Themes: steady in the middle; marked contrasts; various groups; up and down.
148
Symbol: head of violin
(see No. 301)

145

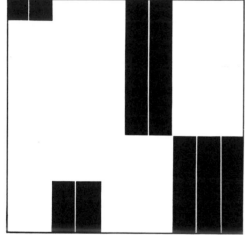

146

147

148

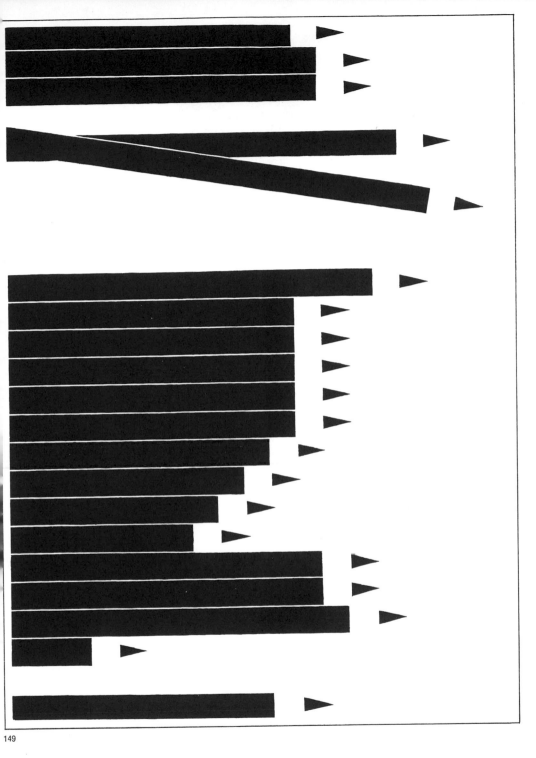

149

150–153: Continuation of exercises
No. 144–147. Variations in the extern.
shape and thickness of the bar.

150
Design for a poster for athletics
151   152
Studies with tools

150

151

152

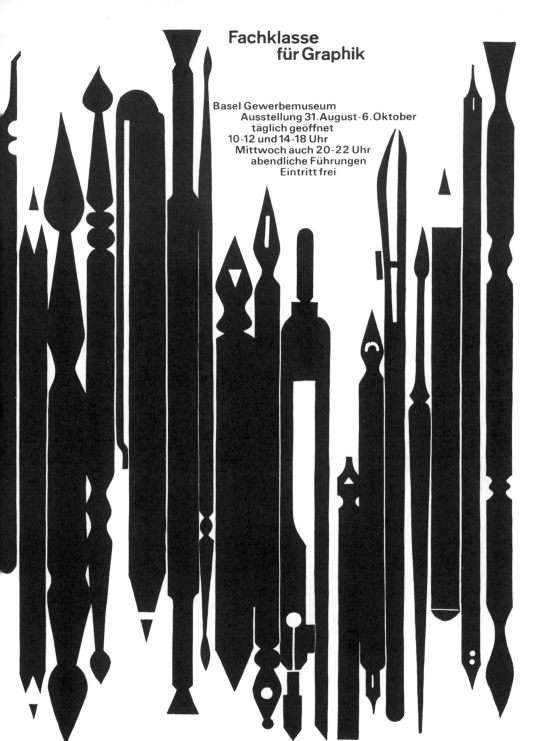

Fachklasse
für Graphik

Basel Gewerbemuseum
Ausstellung 31. August - 6. Oktober
täglich geöffnet
10-12 und 14-18 Uhr
Mittwoch auch 20-22 Uhr
abendliche Führungen
Eintritt frei

53

154

155
Poster for children's traffic school.
The rush of traffic is contrasted with
the quietness of the pedestrian
crosswalk. (Photo and drawing)

155

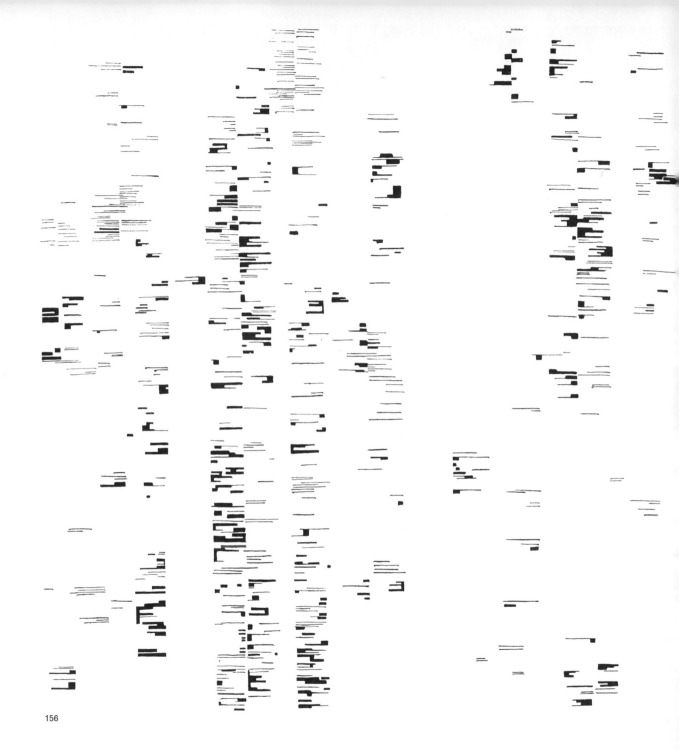

156

156
Transposition exercise from nature:
birch-tree trunks. The verticals
remain in spite of the marked way
in which the horizontals are broken
up. (Pen drawing)
157
Poster for zippers (Drawn on film)

158

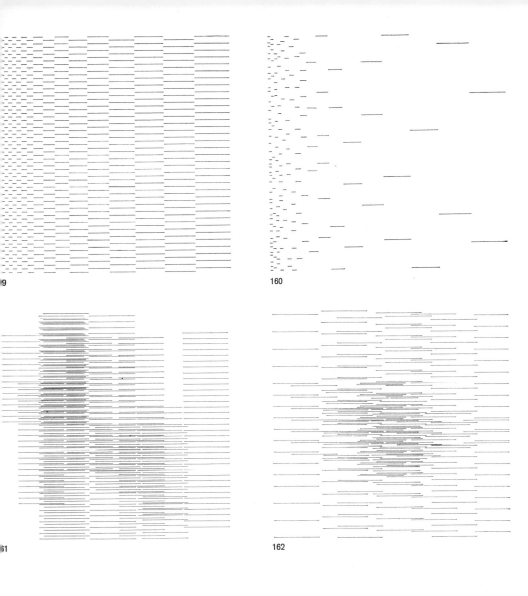

159

160

161

162

161  162  163
Grid studies with the horizontal line.
The overlapping of the lines and
the graded values of grey thus
obtained reinforce the impression of
acceleration. At the same time an
illusion of depth is created.

163

**Mustermesse Halle 6  Geöffnet 1.-20. Juni**
**14-17.30 Uhr, sonntags geschlossen, Eintritt frei**

# Kinderverkehrsgarten

164
Poster for children's traffic school
(Drawn on film)

164

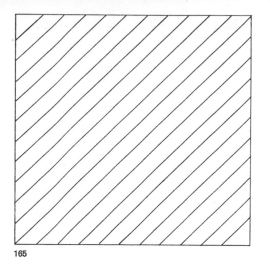

165

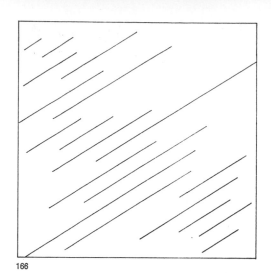

166

165
The pronounced slant of the line
gives it dynamic qualities.
166  167
The impression of dynamic force is
still further enhanced when the line
are of unequal length or placed
with unequal distances between ther

167

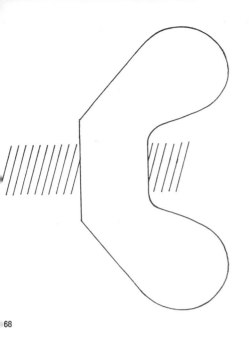

The slant of a regular sequence
of lines evokes turning sensations.
In No. 169 the principle of the double
function already employed in No. 132
is taken a step further.
170
Study with slanting letters

68

169

170

103

171

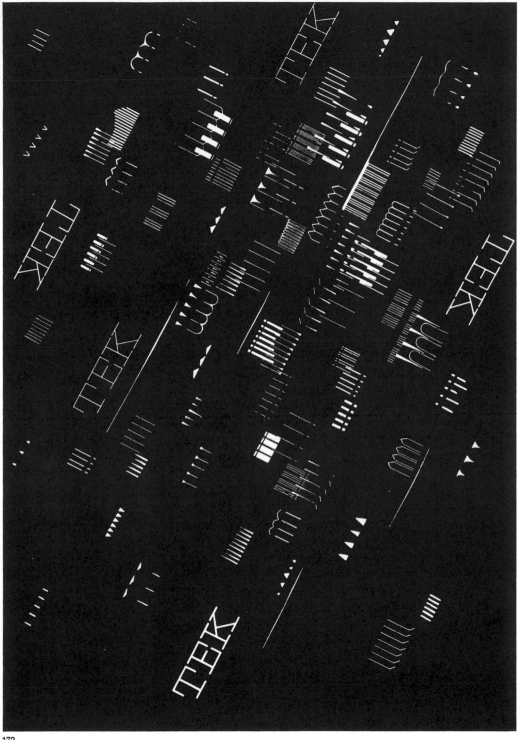

172
Poster for tooth-brushes
(Drawn on film)

172

173

174
Variation of No. 153. The inclined
position of the objects gives added
life to the composition.

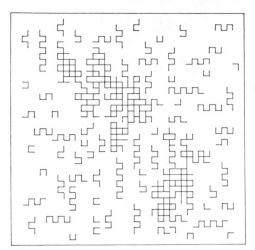

175

175 176 177 178 179 180
181 182
Previously the studies have been
based initially on the autonomous
line. Now a new feature is introduced as vertical, horizontal and
oblique lines are made to meet
(angle). In these grid studies the
most original structures are created
almost spontaneously.

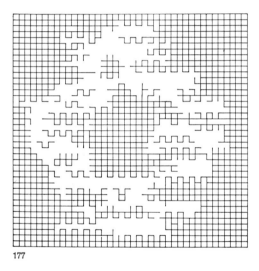

176

177

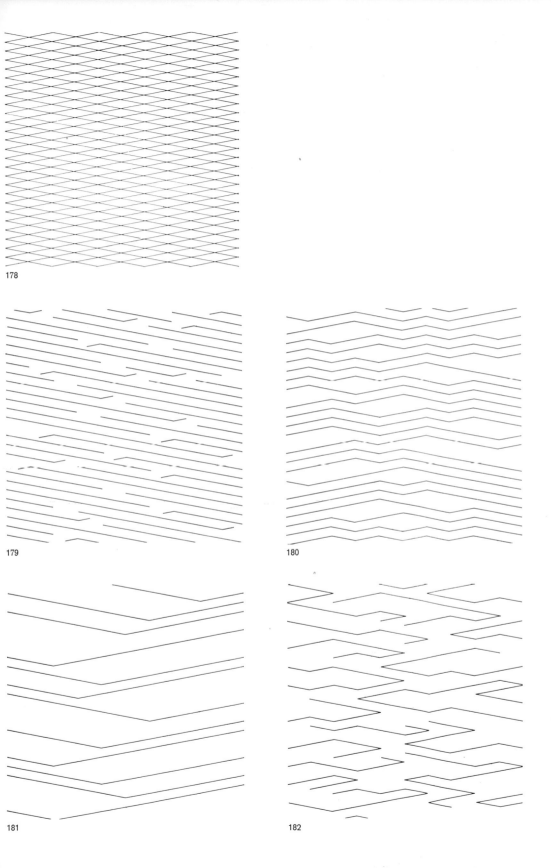

178

179

180

181

182

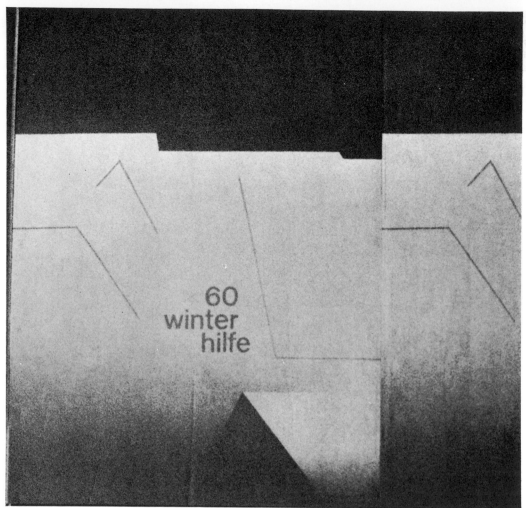

183
Poster for "Winter Aid" (Lithograph)
184
Study with angles of 30°, 45°,
60°, 90°, 120°

183

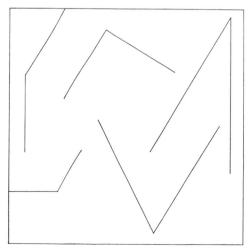

184

Box for insecticide. The actual
sizes of the various angles on the
lateral faces of the cube alter
depending on the viewpoint of the
onlooker. In this particular instance
the illusion of swarming insects is
intensified.

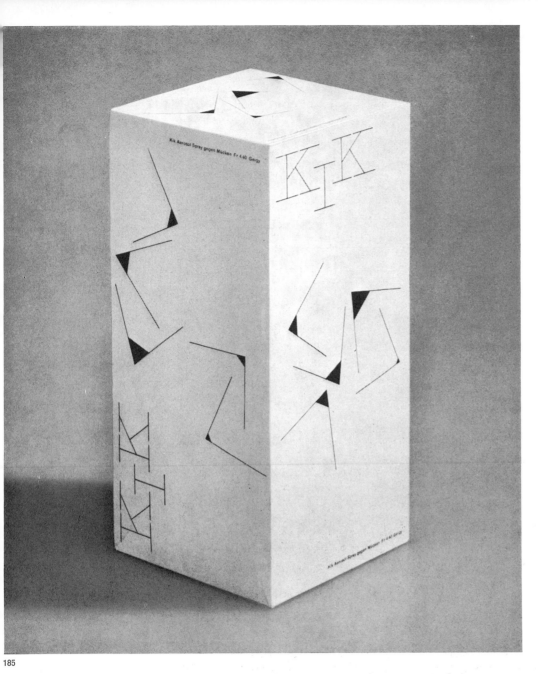

185

winter
hilfe
1960

186

186
Poster for "Winter Aid". The varying
thicknesses of the legs of the angles
create an impression of jingle,
glitter and tingle.

Competition for an inn sign "The Sun". The various angles meeting at the center evoke the idea of rays. The impression is intensified by the play of light and shade.
(Wood relief)

87

188
Draft for a music poster. The various
groups of angles interpenetrate.
Associations with musical scores and
sounds.
189
Study with group movements.
Angles, centers, turning motions,
radiating powers form the basis of
the exercice. (Drawn on film)

188

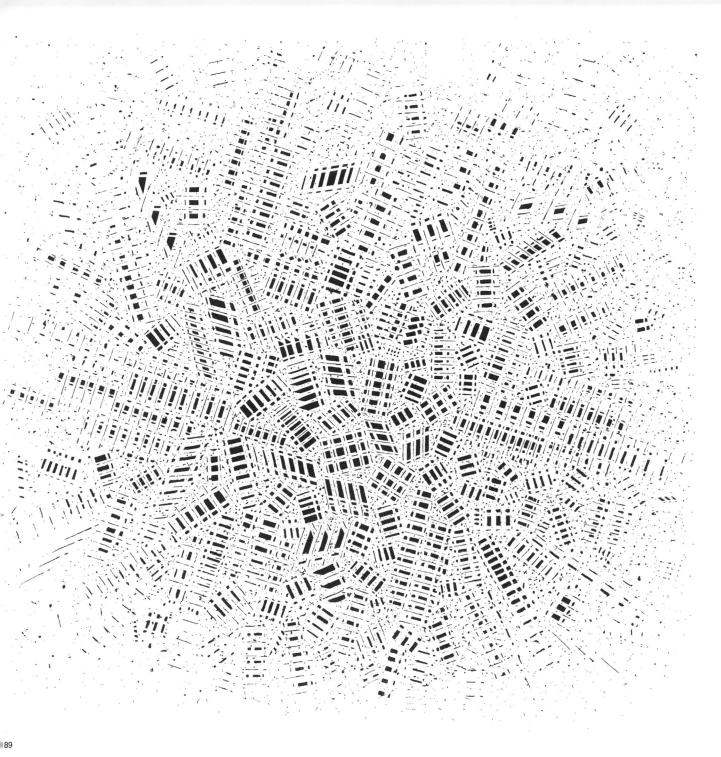

89

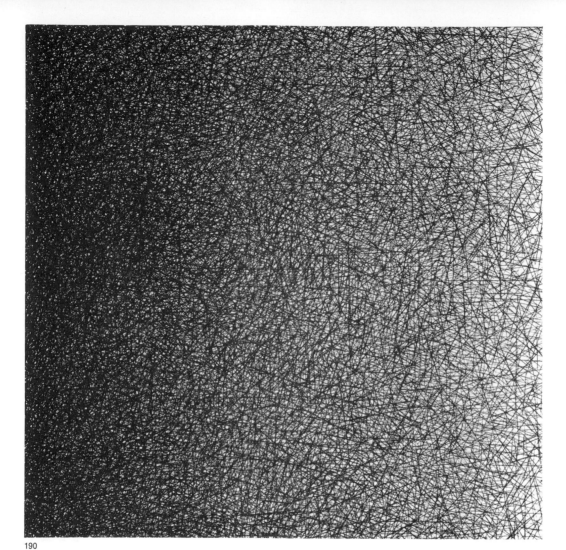

190

190 191
Texture studies. The lines are
condensed into a network. The
direction of the individual line
is lost.
192
Study with scattered needles

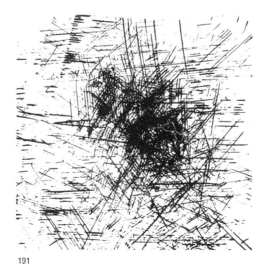

191

116

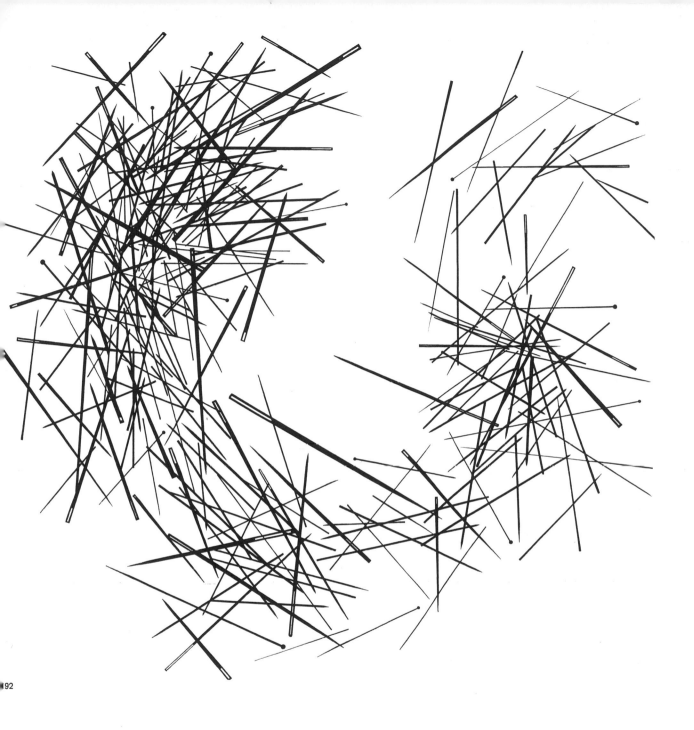

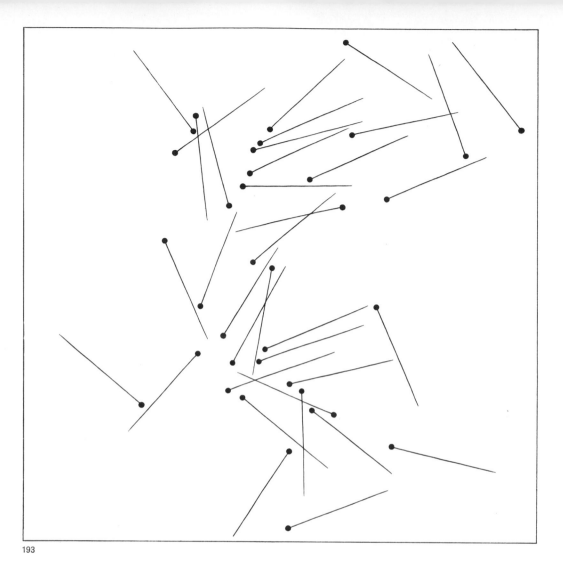

193
Study with scattered pins
194
Study with scattered paper clips

193

194

195
Box for fly-killer.
Scattering exercise on a solid.
196
Advertisement for mosquito-killer

195

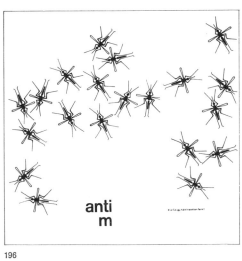

196

197

198

199

Grouping exercises with pen-nibs.
Themes: simple contrasted arrangement (198); loose scattering (199);
densification (197); compaction (200).

200

201
Design for an ant-killer box.
Wrapper unfolded flat.
202
View showing two sides of the box

201

202

203
Side of the box. In the previous
studies in densification the straight
line formed the basis. Already in
No. 197—200, and more pronouncedly
still in this ant-killer box, the curved
line has been added.

Neocid    Geigy<sup>R</sup>

203

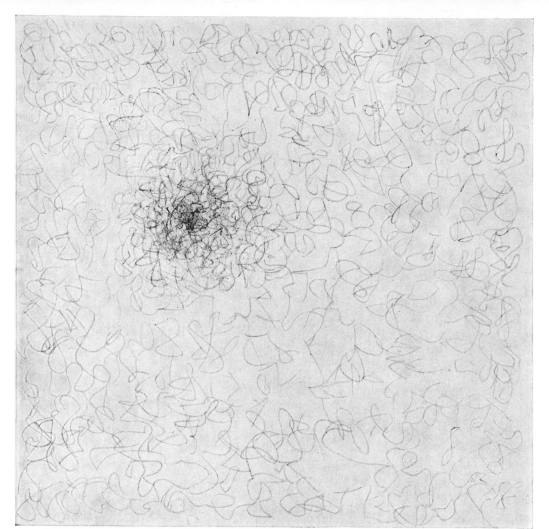

204

204
Scribbling exercise. The surface is covered with uniform scribbling movements which start from a center and work outwards. (Chalk lithograph)
205
Scribbling exercise with a hard brush (Lithograph)

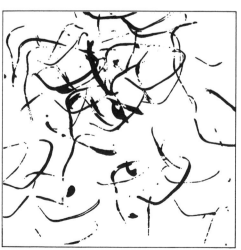

205

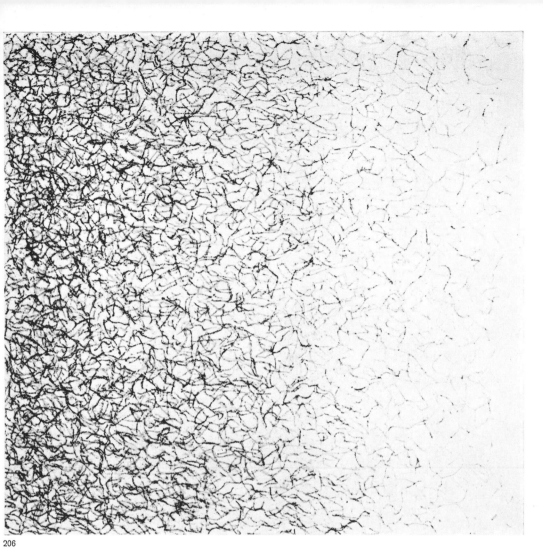

206
Scribbling exercise. The scribbling
movements fade away from left to
right. (Chalk lithograph)

206

207

207
Vigorous spontaneous movements
with crayon (Lithograph)
208
Slow development of a winding line
with a fine pen

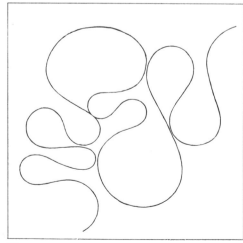

208

Line exercises with paths of motion.
In both exercises the thickness and
curvature of the lines are varied.
In No. 210 there is also a gradation
of tone value.

210

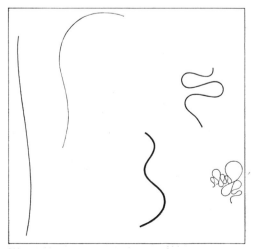

211

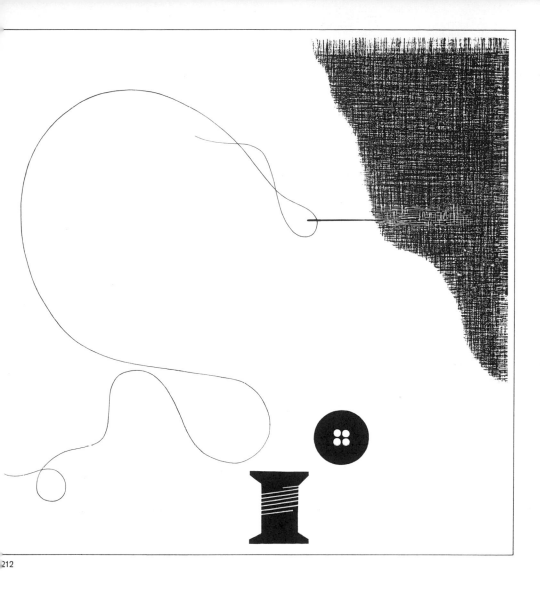

212

Confrontation

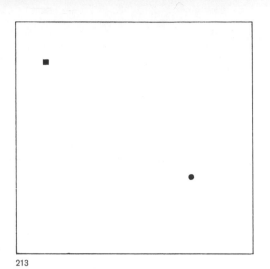

213

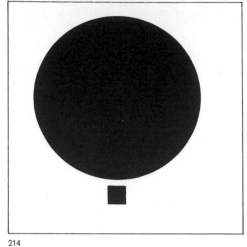

214

213–218: Confrontation studies

213
Because of their smallness and isolated position the two elements – round-square dot – do not appear as a contrasting pair.
214
The confrontation is made clear.
215
The two elements merge from below and above.
216
The square dot expands to its utmost limit. The round dot dwindles towards its center.
217
The two elements merge into each other form all four sides.
218
The two elements overlap. Residual forms appear.

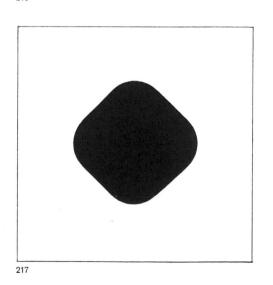

215

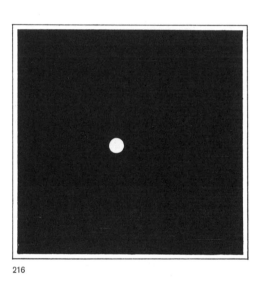

216

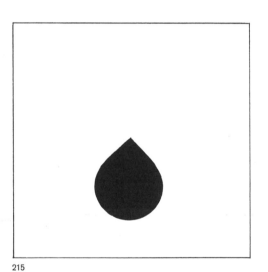

217

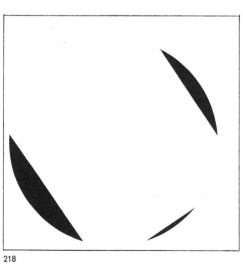

218

219
Poster for children's traffic school
(Combination linocut and
typography)

kinderverkehrsgarten

mustermesse halle 9
14. sept.-3. okt.
täglich geoffnet
14.00-17.00 Uhr
sonntags geschlossen

219

220

Exercises with playing card figures. Straight and curved lines confront one another with the addition of light and dark in No. 221.

221

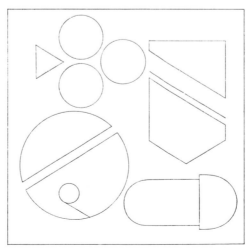

222

135

223

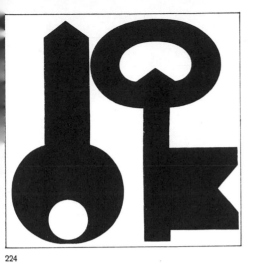

224

225

226

227

228

229

229  230  231
Confrontation studies. Dot and line
and various objects are juxtaposed
in contrast; in No. 230 and 231 there
is also the element of lettering.
232
Confrontation study: horizontal–
vertical, dot–line, black–white.

230

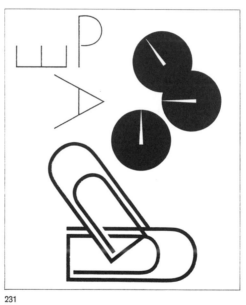

231

232

233

233 234 235 236 237
Designs for a stamp competition.
Interplay between object and
lettering.

234

235

236

237

238
Poster design for a department store
Objects with different pictorial
qualities form a unified pattern
together with the lettering.
(Linocut)

238

140

239

240

Poster for Jeunesse Musicale. Here
dot–line, black–white, narrow-wide,
repetition of dot–repetition of line,
and two oblique lines confront one
another in the general pattern.

241

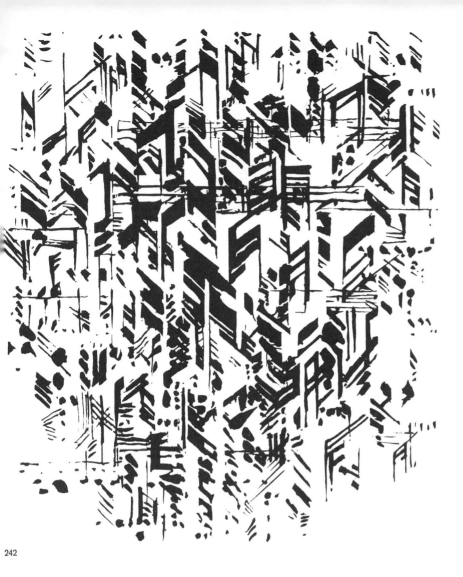

242

242
Several contrasting elements are
linked together in a rapidly executed
process.
243
Symbol for the «Crown Hotel»
244
Symbol for the Music Institute

243

244

143

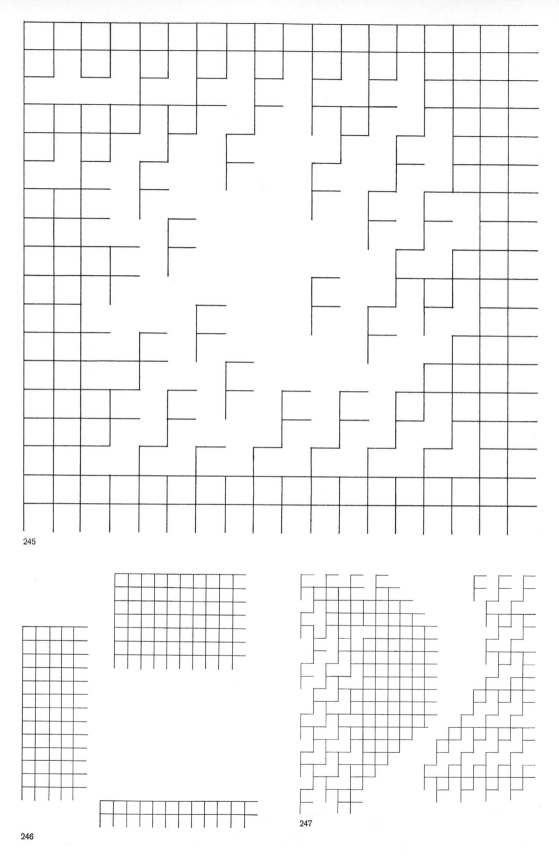

245 246 247
Grid studies. The letter F is
separated out of the grid.

245

246

247

146

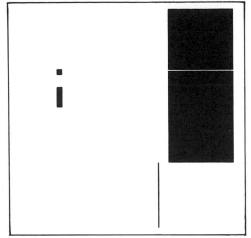

248 249 250 251 252 253
Composition and motion studies
with the letter i

48

249

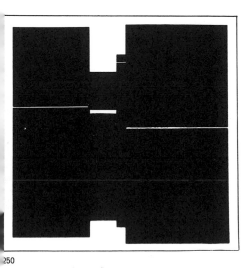

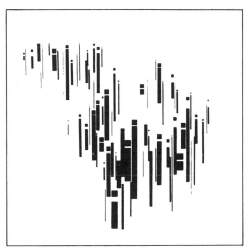

250

251

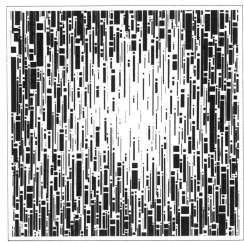

252

253

147

254
Composition study with the letter i.
Lines and dots are grouped accord-
ing to various laws.
255
Composition study with the letter H

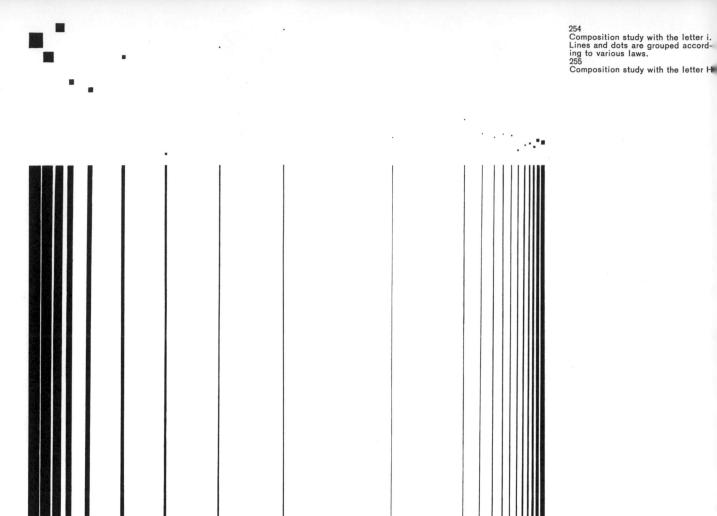

254

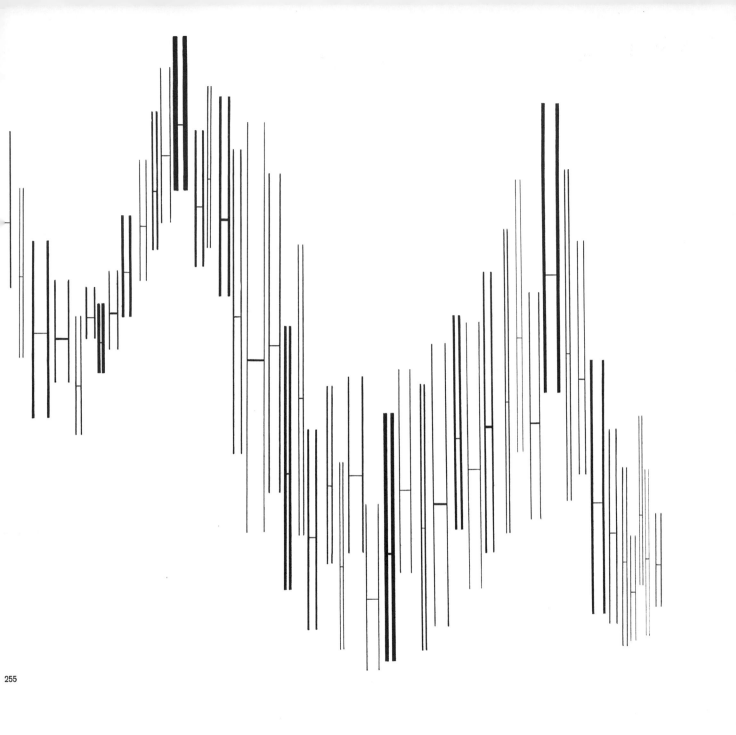

255

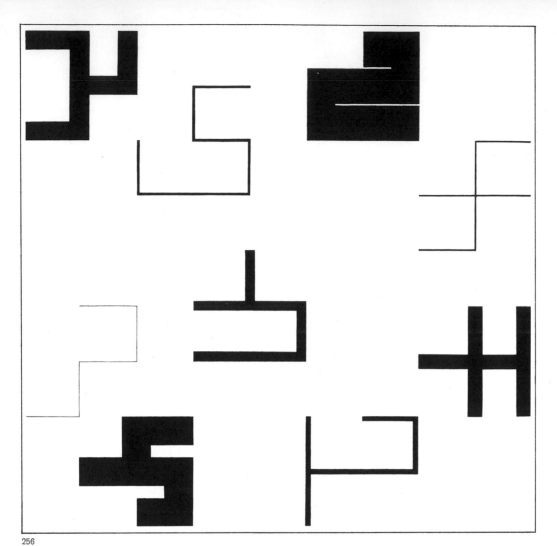

256

256
Vertical and horizontal lines meet
and intersect. Differences in the
thickness of the line produce a new
white linear value.
257
Three letter H's showing extreme
variations of form

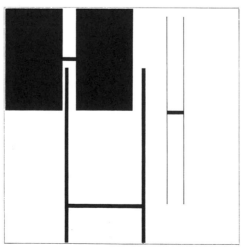

257

150

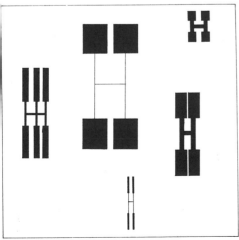

258
Five letters made up of horizontal
and vertical lines meet. Their weight
is determined by their size and the
thickness of their lines.
259
Study with the letter H.
Dot shapes on lines.

260  261  262
Studies with the letter E. No. 261
provides the starting point for these
studies. In No. 260 the dark background shades away from the left s
that the two E's on the right side
lose definition against the lightene
background. The reverse process
is found in No. 262.

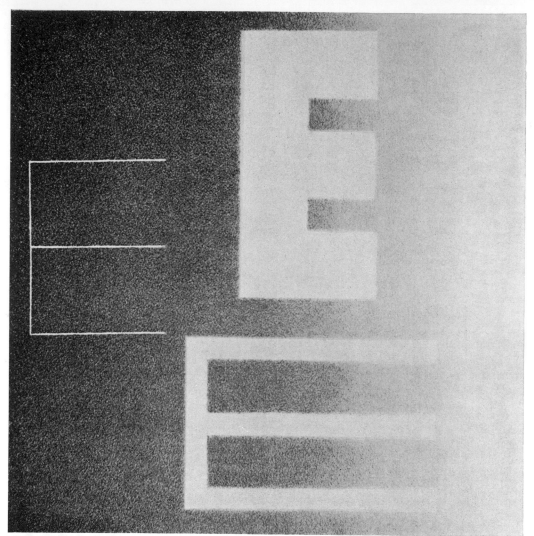

260

261

262

263

264

263
Letter F's are linked together into a
total form.
264
Study with letter F.
Four F's graded in tone value.

153

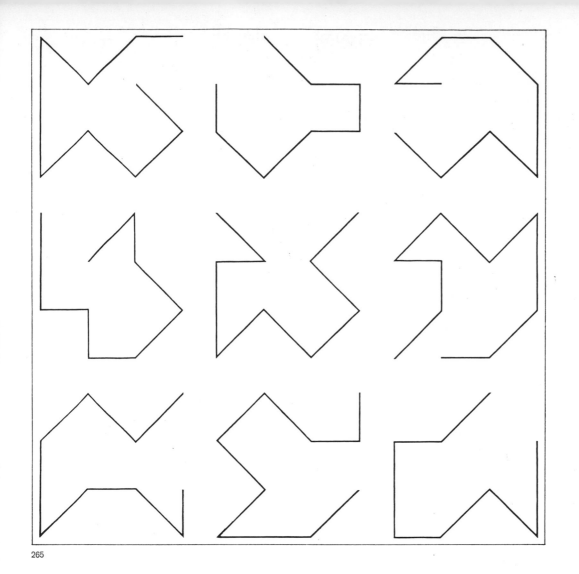

265

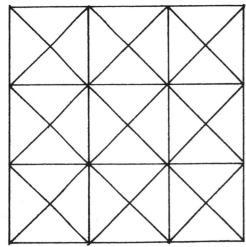

266

265 266
The diagonal line is a structural
element in letters and imparts
movement to their form. Various
figures have been separated out of
grid No. 266 and linked together
in a composition in No. 265.
267
Symbol for the steel construction
firm of Suter

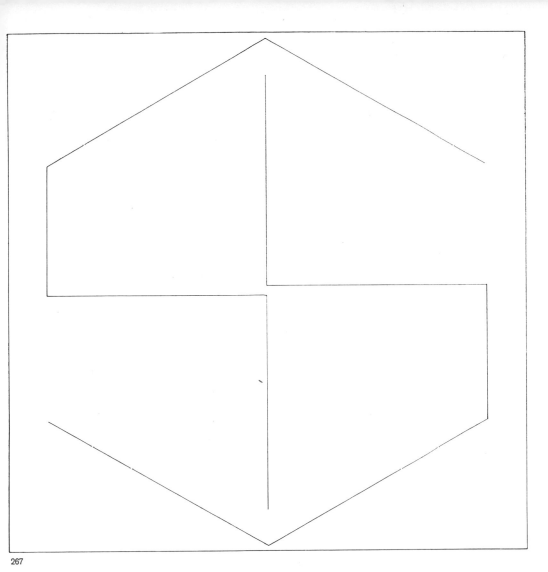

267

268

269

268
Signs resembling letters are separated out from a geometrical figure (two intersecting diagonals in a square).
269
Vertical, horizontal and oblique elements form letters of different weights which are grouped together to form an unit.
270
Letters of the alphabet which are formed of horizontal, vertical or diagonal lines.
271
Alternative version of No. 267

270

271

272
Container for cleaning agent
273
Symbol for musical congress

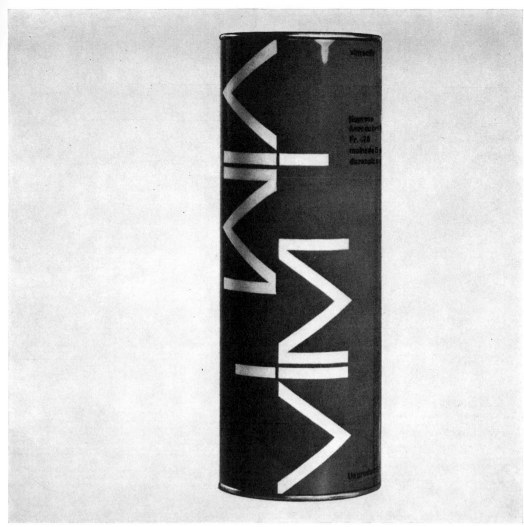

272

273

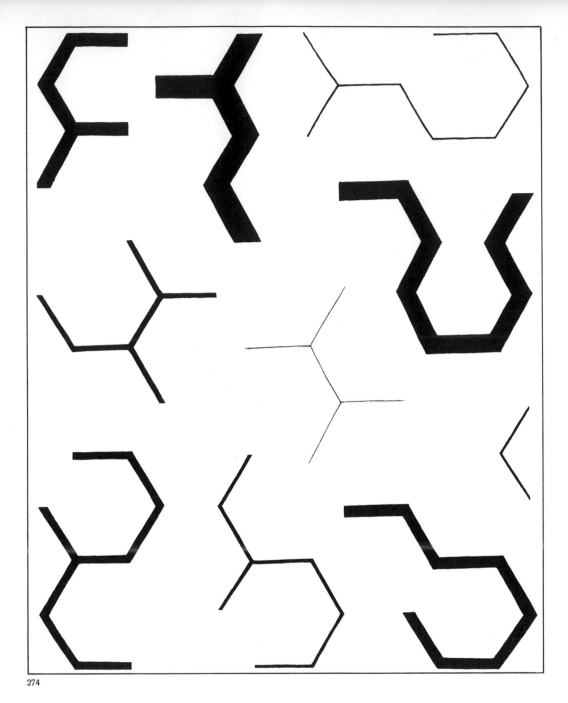

274

275

276
Symbol picture. Basic elements of
our letters: circle, square, traingle.
277
Symbol for Dalang, manufacturer of
alimentary pastes

276

277

EF ED EA 1E

278
Study with the letter E, which comes
into contact with letters of a different
structure. In some cases curiously
harmonious figures are obtained.
Sometimes the figures actually form
a combination of letters which can
be used as a logotype. Examples:
No. 277, 279.
279
Logotype for the Basle electrical
power company. A suitable arrangement of the lines symbolizes processes arising in the application of
electricity. See also No. 46.

EX ES EI UE

EJ EO EL YE

EN EK ET 3E

278

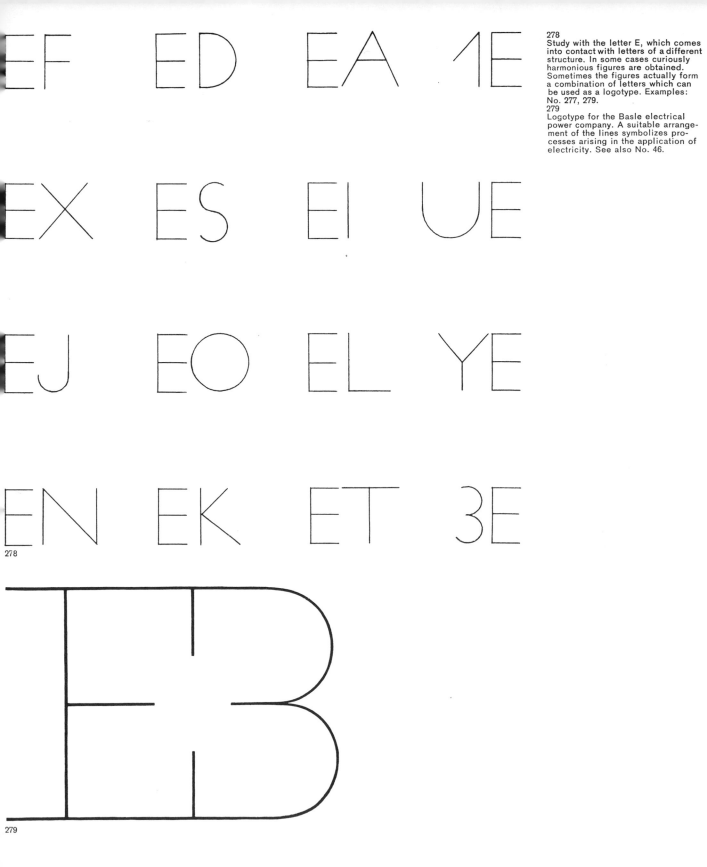

279

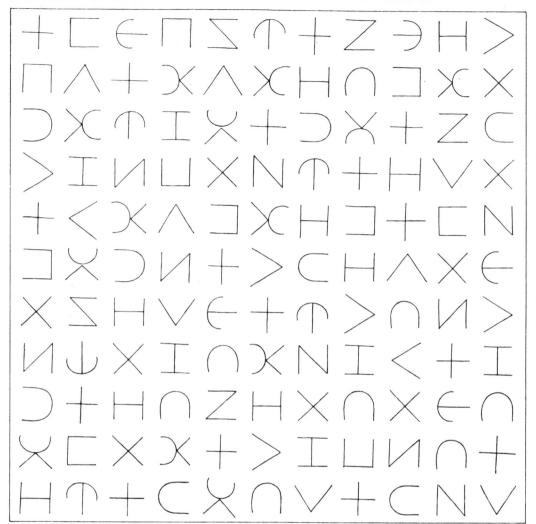

280
Composition of existing and possibl[e]
new letter symbols
281
Numerals picture. The same numeral[s]
join together and are emphasized by
their diagonal run.
282
Roman lettering (Pencil)

280

234567890 1
34567890 12
4567890 123
567890 1234
67890 12345
7890 123456
890 1234567

281

162

QVI MOS FVIT APVD VETERES NEOS OBSCVRIS NEOS
PAVCIS EXEMPLIS COMPROBATVS VTI SIVE PROPRIA SV
SIVE AB ALIS CODITA MONVMETA IN PVBLICVM
PRODIRE ABSOS COMENDATIONE NON PATERENTVR EVM
MIHI QVOS SEQVENDVM NVNC ESSE IVDICAVI EXISTIMANS
MEA OFFITIVM NON ILLIBERALE OPERA PRAETIVM
MINIME VLGARE HOC MODO FACTVRVM ESSE
SIQVIDEM OFFICIVM NVLLVM MAIVS HABERVS DEBET
QVAM VTI POSTERORVM HOMINVM CVRAM HABEAMVS
NON MINORE QVAM DE NOBIS MAIORES HABVERVRVNT
ET HVERVSCE REIOCCASIO AVT ALIA NON EST AVT
CERTE NVLLA POITOR EST QVAM QVE IN ADOLESCENTIE
ANIMIS INSTITVTVM EST EXEMPLA COMPARANDA SVNT
QVE AD IMITATIONEM FORMANDAM IVENIBVS
VTILITER APTE PROPONI POSINT HAEC NVSQVAM
ALIVNDE RECTIVS PENTENTVR QVEX EORVM AVTORVM
ORDINE QVI INTER CAETEROS FVI GENERIS SEMPER
SVMMI EXTITERVNT OVELA CERTE GENVS NVLLA LAVDATIO
POSTVLAT SED A SEMETIPSO SVAM LVCEM HABET EXVE
VERO GENERE ANTIQVISIMV HVNC VATEM ESSE ECQVIS NON
AFFIRMARE VOLET SANE AVTORES ALIAB ANTIQVITATE
ALIA DOCTRINA AVT A GENERE IPSO IN QVO VERSANTVR
COMENDARE SOLET ANTICELIT THEOCRITVS FVI GENERIS
HISCE VNIVERFIS NOMINIBVS ALIOS OMNES CARMINIS HVIVS
TITVLVS EST BVCCOLICA ANTIQVISIMVM PORRO SCRIBEDI
GENVS ISTVD SOLEM ESSE CONFIRMAT ORIGINIS ANTIQVITAS
QVAE DIVTVRNITATE TEMPORIS IPSAM QVOS HOMINVM
MEMORIAM PRAEVERTISSE VIDET QVADO ADEO INTER SCRIPTO

282

283
Harmony of various block capitals
on a box. The individual letters are
designed in highly contrasted forms.
Block letters are particularly suitable
for this purpose.

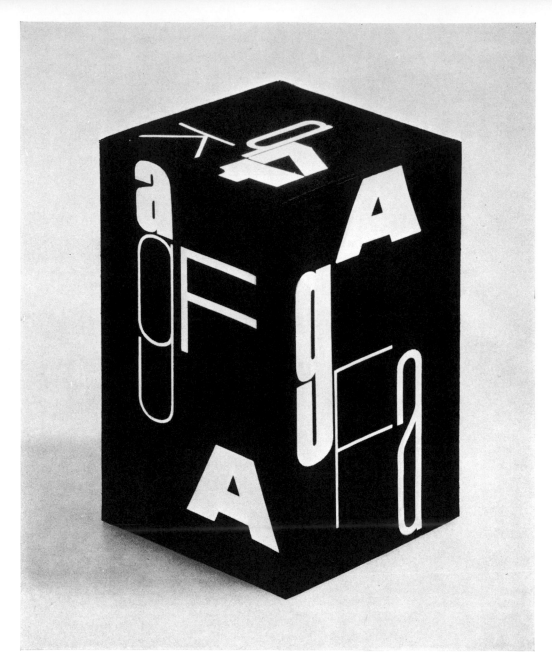

283

284

284
Letter composition. Pieces of wood
provide the basic material and are
combined, cut out, hollowed out and
notched to produce the three-
dimensional letter.
285
Logotype for the Allgemeine Musik-
gesellschaft Basle. The three basic
elements of circle, square and
triangle make a distinctive symbol.

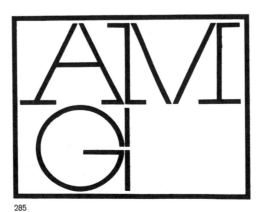

285

286
Poster for an electric light bulb
manufacturer. The association with
the electric light bulb is elicited by
the contrast of the black background
and the bright lines and dots.
(Linocut)

287
Package for an electric light bulb
manufacturer. In a similar manner
the ductus of the classic letters
symbolizes here light and luminosity.
288   289
The spatial arrangement of the letters
repeats the structure of the filaments
and thus symbolizes the radiation
of light. The insertion of the fine
crossed lines in No. 288 underlines
the subtlety of the material and
process.

287

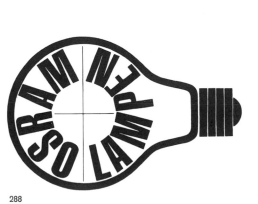

288

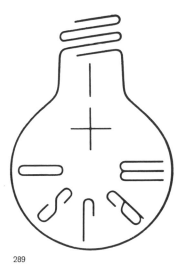

289

Composition study with letters and a numeral. Large and small curves, long and short straight lines compose into a positive statement.

290

Charity poster for Caritas. The
diagonal lines bring life and activity
into the composition. By thickening
the lines as compared with No. 290,
the black background is mobilized
and brought out of its passive role.

291

292

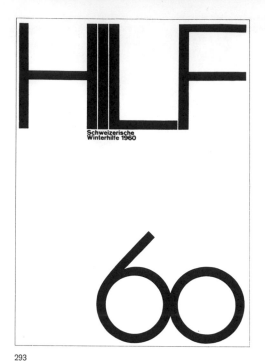

293

292  293  294  295  298
Five competition designs for a
"Winter Aid" poster

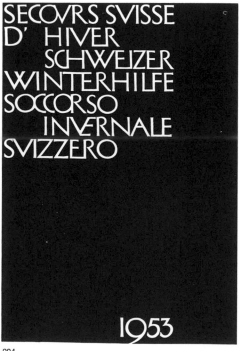

294

295

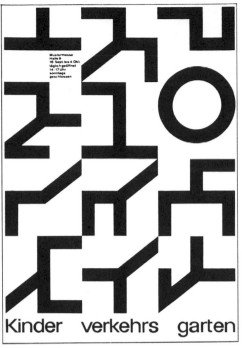

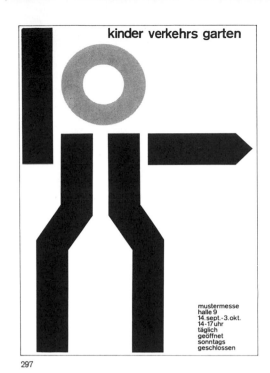

kinder verkehrs garten

Kinder verkehrs garten

296

297

296 297 299
Three competition designs for a
children's traffic school poster

298

299

300

301

The printing technique is
mentioned in the captions only
when it has a particular bearing
on the creation of the work shown.